ALIGNED

THE SURPRISING FACTORS DRIVING THE BUSINESS VALUE OF IT

Simon Chapleau

ISBN-13: 978-1508602125

ISBN-10: 1508602123

Dedication

To the entire Green Elephant Team. This project wouldn't have been possible without your valued contribution.

Table of contents

Introduction

"How do I know if I'm delivering business value?"

It was in 2007, in the departure lounge of the Las Vegas airport, when I ran into Marc, the Chief Information Officer (CIO) of a large pharmaceutical organization who had just attended the same conference I had. At the time, I was working as a director for Gartner, a large information technology (IT) management consulting company. I had worked with Marc on several occasions, helping him develop an IT strategic plan and service strategy. I was familiar with his organization, having regular contacts with its team and the business. Marc was definitely in the top five CIOs that I knew. Few people showed his vision and leadership. In fact, in only three years, he had completely transformed his organization, taking a disparate bunch of services with a bad reputation and forming them into a cohesive, focused team.

"I have all sorts of metrics, performance indicators, dashboards," Marc told me, "yet I feel I'm completely in the dark about this. How do I know if I'm heading in the right direction?"

Being the management consultant with all the answers, I was surprised by his question. "I don't think any metrics can tell you that," I answered. "I guess the only way to know for sure is to ask the business."

This answer left Marc somewhat dissatisfied. He would have liked to have had a metric, an indicator that would track his business's value and provide something to manage against. Of course, he had budgets, benchmarks, and project dashboards, but nothing close to business value.

This conversation left me frustrated as well. How credible is business value as a concept if you can't even measure it?

A few years later, I became even more preoccupied with this concept. I had become the CIO of a traditional, family-owned manufacturing company that was nothing more than a collection of regional plants and offices with little in common. The president wanted to modernize the company by establishing common systems and processes. I thought it would provide not only a great challenge, but also an excellent opportunity to test many of the theories I had developed as a consultant. But the same question started nagging at me again: how will I know if I'm delivering business value?

Two years later, our project team did the impossible, delivering a complex Enterprise Resource Planning (ERP) transformation project on time and within budget. We also succeeded in taking users from a manual, labor-intensive process to an automated, real-time system. The team won prizes and was featured in several industry magazines. We were asked to speak at conferences and share our best practices.

But transforming the organization came at a cost: the business hated us.

We had imposed so many new ways of working and so many new technologies that we had turned their work upside down. We had removed all their expertise and experience and automated it into a computer system. I had been so focused on delivery that I had forgotten that I wouldn't be the one living with these systems for years to come—the users would be.

So, if driving business transformation and improving operation aren't driving value, what is? Why are some IT departments so successful at delivering value while others seem to fail miserably? Is it possible to replicate these conditions from one organization to another?

These questions became the focus of my research and work. I was convinced that IT departments could contribute to the success of their organization and that they could help it become more productive, competitive, and innovative. I believed that IT could be the driving force behind this transformation.

As part of the Business Value of IT Research, we analyzed, surveyed, and interviewed over two hundred organizations. We talked to IT departments, users, and business executives. We talked to both successful and not-so-successful IT departments. We tried to cover as many industries and sizes as possible.

Our five years of research yielded many surprising conclusions, but the most important conclusion of all was the discovery that delivering business value was within reach of ALL IT departments—that it wasn't a factor of the industry, of the size of the team, or even of the IT budget. We also learned that, although delivering value is quite simple, it is not easy.

We're hoping to share those conclusions and approaches with you, so that you, too, can deliver amazing business value.

The Business Value of IT research project

I spent more than ten years at Gartner as a consultant, helping several companies make the most of their IT departments. As such, I had the chance to collaborate with various types of organizations, and I was always surprised to see the differences in how the businesses perceived their IT departments.

Some of the IT departments were real partners, participating in the decision-making and strategy-setting process. They were the example to follow, doing everything right.

Yet, some other organizations followed all the best practices Gartner recommended. They put in place countless processes, methodologies, and whatnot to become better partners, and still had terrible reputations within the organization. Value was not only not recognized in these cases, but the IT department was almost a laughing stock.

The project started in 2012 with one key objective: to measure the business value of IT departments. It was a massive undertaking. We set out to survey over 150,000 users, business managers, and IT leaders. We conducted hundreds of interviews. The goal was to get a balanced perspective on each organization: IT leadership, IT employees, business leaders, and users.

To aid our work, we borrowed from the marketing world, which has a long track record in evaluating and measuring business value. We adapted these marketing concepts to the context of IT departments, which are "monopolies"; that is, users don't have a choice.

The stages of business value

While measuring the business value of the IT departments, we noticed that they tended to aggregate themselves into four different groups.

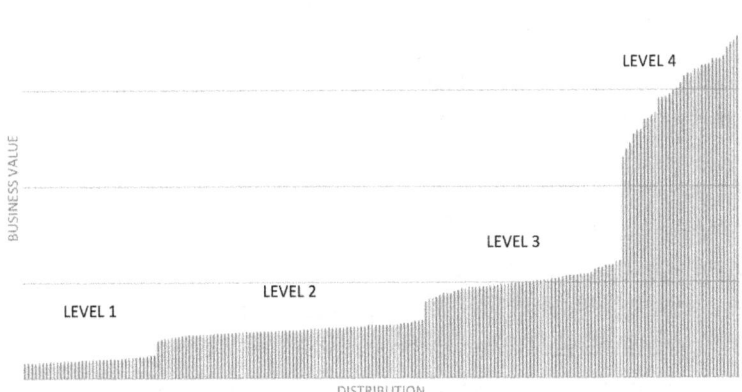

BUSINESS VALUE DISTRIBUTION

After analyzing these groupings, we saw that they represented four different levels of evolution:

Level 1. These IT departments focus almost exclusively on managing technology. They contribute little business value because the business sees them as either a commodity or an obstacle.

Level 2. The second level tends to focus on delivering projects. Their value is higher because they contribute to changing the organization. However, their focus on projects tends to lead to poor operational performance.

Level 3. The third level tends to be great service managers. Their value comes from being outstanding service managers. They are predictable and can be relied upon.

Level 4. The fourth level, the high-value IT departments, provide value by building individual relationships with all parts of the business and adapting their service model to fit the business's needs.

We expected to see some differences in business value based on the maturity, structure, and budget of IT departments. What we found, instead, were a small group of IT departments that eclipsed everyone else completely in terms of business value. Their contribution was so high that it couldn't be explained by budgets and structure alone. Something else drove their business value. The Level 4 IT departments were in a class of their own.

Level 4 IT departments were also very different from the inside. Their teams were productive, focused, and engaged, with good reputations within the business. The IT teams were involved in many business initiatives, and the IT leaders never seemed surprised by new projects or initiatives. They were always in the know. In short, IT appeared to be embedded in all parts of the business instead of simply being just one supplier amongst others.

We found six factors that distinguish these Level 4 teams from everyone else. Working with our clients, we developed an approach to help IT departments establish these same conditions and become high-value creators as well.

In this book, we'd like to share our findings with you. But first, let's define what *business value* means.

What is business value?
As a middle-aged man trying to stay active, I'd say I'm well-acquainted with Tylenol. In fact, we are best buddies.

But, if you've purchased Tylenol lately, you've seen the price difference between Tylenol and its closest competitor: acetaminophen. The difference is so great that, in some stores, Tylenol is twice as expensive. So, it begs the question: what's the difference between Tylenol and acetaminophen? There is none. Tylenol is acetaminophen with a red coating in a red box. From a pure health perspective, they are identical. And I don't mean similar — they are the exact same thing.

So, why are people ready to pay twice as much to buy Tylenol? Because they trust the brand. Tylenol has evolved as a strong brand in the last decades, to the point where it has replaced the drug's generic name. People go out to buy Tylenol, not acetaminophen.

The value of a brand

The value of a brand can be defined by how much more people are willing to pay simply for the name. Let's take our Tylenol example. Considering that acetaminophen is the exact same thing and sells for half the price of Tylenol, the value of the Tylenol brand is 100 percent more than that of its generic competition. Of course, this is even more apparent in the apparel sector, where Louis Vuitton and Prada accessories sell for thousands of dollars while the cost of manufacturing lingers around the tens of dollars.

Consumers will pay more for branded items for various reasons: status, social acceptance, and prestige, for example.

But, in the business world, would anyone pay more for a brand? After all, businesses focus on cost optimization, right?

Well, the main reason businesses pay more for a brand is because:

- They trust that the brand has the required knowledge.
- They trust that the brand has the experience.
- They trust that the brand has their best interests at heart.
- They trust that the brand will evolve with their ongoing needs.

The business value of IT is its brand

To define it, *business value* is IT's brand. It is the amount of money your organization would be willing to pay to use your services, above the price of the pure commodity.

Why would users get their services from you instead of an external provider? If the only reason is because they have to, then chances are your brand (and business value) is negative. People would pay someone else more to receive the same services.

But, if the business is willing to pay more to get services from your IT department, then they probably put a premium on the services they are receiving from you.

Brands are based on perceptions

What if I were to ask you which brand makes a better coffee: Starbucks or Dunkin' Donuts? Chances are, you will answer Starbucks. After all, Starbucks coffee is more expensive, one of the most efficient indicators of a brand's prestige.

But blind tests have shown that people tend to prefer Dunkin' Donuts' coffee over Starbucks. Dunkin' Donuts' coffee is regarded as less bitter and more enjoyable overall. Yet, their coffee is about half the price of Starbucks.

The same thing holds true for business value. Your IT department might be working very hard and delivering amazing service. Yet, if people have the wrong perception of your service (or are not aware of it), it won't translate into business value. This is why managing perceptions is as important as delivering great service.

The brand of the Transportation Security Administration (TSA)

If you have recently flown by air in the United States, you are probably familiar with the Transportation Security Administration (TSA). TSA is the agency responsible for keeping us safe while traveling. Of course, they do so by making sure we are thirsty by removing our water bottles before they check our baggage.

TSA suffers from a pretty bad reputation. Surveys show that 85 percent of frequent flyers give the TSA a fair or poor rating. They find their operations inefficient, their security rules absurd, and their agents arrogant.

After all, who would be dumb enough to bring a weapon aboard a plane? Well, in 2013, that would have been 1,813 persons, or five

8

persons a day—and 81 percent of the guns seized were loaded. Of course, not everyone is a terrorist, but that still represents a large number of weapons. And that's not counting the number of knives, explosives, and medieval maces they confiscated!

But let's be honest—the TSA has a pretty thankless job. It has to choose between annoying millions of legitimate passengers with invasive and disruptive security procedures or taking the risk that a potential threat gets aboard a plane. And, of course, if the TSA softens its procedures and an incident happens, no one will be on its side to defend it.

The TSA is an example of an organization that suffers from major brand issues. The business value it provides is undeniable, yet its contribution goes unrecognized.

The framework

We wrapped the concepts in this book around a simple framework that we call the *business value engine*. Trying to meet Marc's desire for a business value metric (I'm only ten years late, Marc, sorry), we developed a way to quantify business value. Our method provides a simple way of explaining what drives business value. In the process of our research, we found six main characteristics that influence the perception of the business value of IT:

1. Deliver the Basics

We were surprised to see the impact that basic IT services had on the perception of business value. We would have thought that providing computers, Internet access, and help-desk support would be a commodity service by now, but, in fact, it is quite the opposite. Successful IT departments use basic IT services as a mechanism to gain and demonstrate their credibility and build relationships with the users.

2. Engage the users

Users are a captive audience, the consumers of a monopoly. They cannot go elsewhere to get their services. So, what does it matter if they are satisfied or not? Actually, it matters a great deal. Successful IT departments work hard not only to deliver great service, but also to engage the users so they get maximum use out of the systems available to them.

3. Play your role

We anticipated that governance would play a major role when it came to business value and alignment. But, in fact, governance had little to do with it. How the IT team behaved compared to what the business expected played the biggest role. Sometimes alignment means doing more, but sometimes it means doing less.

4. Create partnerships

Successful IT departments aren't happy simply playing the role expected by the business; they also change expectations. They work hard to build credibility and earn the right to play a major role in the direction and orientation of their organization.

5. Fewer but better

Although technical skills are important, we were surprised to find that customer service skills were even more important. In fact, successful IT departments hire based on attitude and then train their staff in technical skills. And they keep on training for attitude.

6. Goldilocks processes

Finally, successful IT departments build processes to help the users, not only to help themselves. They do not transfer the work to the users or require them to fill out paperwork before they can talk with them. Instead, the processes they put in place are meant to make their users' lives easier.

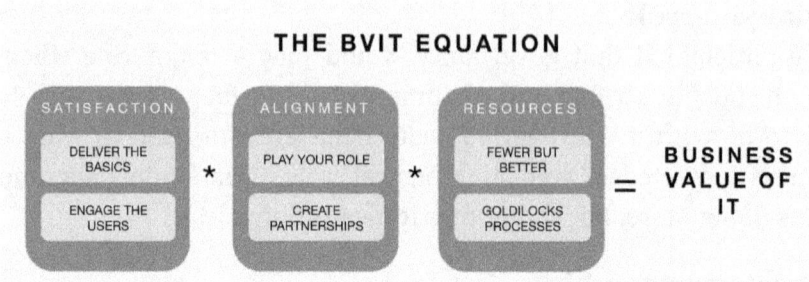

What was not a factor

Most interestingly, we also discovered that some factors had little to no impact on business value:

1. Technology

Despite the amount of time and money that goes into selecting the right technology, we found no correlation between the type of technology used and business value. We didn't even find any correlation between the age of the technology and value.

2. IT budget

We found no correlation between the IT budget and the perceived business value. IT departments with high budgets weren't more likely to provide business value. Value was accessible even for departments with severe budget constraints. That was one of our biggest discoveries. This means that business value is not a matter of how much money you have, but how you spend it. You cannot buy your way to business value.

3. Governance

Governance is all the rage in the industry journals when we talk about alignment. But, surprisingly, governance wasn't really a factor. We've seen IT departments with an IT monarchy (IT decides everything) provide amazing value. In fact, we've found that leading IT departments do their work before it hits governance. They work using influence and leadership to align the business before governance even comes into play. For them, governance is mostly an approval process.

4. Outsourcing

If service is so important, then does it stand to reason that outsourcing will have a negative impact on business value? Not at all. Leading IT departments are as likely to run operations in-house as outsourcing it. What differentiates leading IT departments is the level of effort they put into managing their outsourcing relationship. They don't outsource their problems.

It's about partnership

At the end of the day, business value is about partnership—and no partnerships are equal. Successful IT departments adapt themselves to their partners and influence their partners to change. Just like any relationship, no single formula exists. But there are guidelines.

I hope this book will inspire you to develop deeper, more meaningful partnerships; that it will serve as a source of inspiration for you and your team; and finally, that it will play a small role in your future success.

1. Deliver the Basics

Mary: Your typical user

It is a Monday morning in a typical finance department. Mary is coming back from a nice, relaxing weekend with her family and getting settled for the upcoming week. As usual, she starts her computer, which she closes diligently every Friday night. IT has told her that she doesn't need to do this, but she feels that it is a nice way to finish the work week. Close the computer, close the work week.

But, as usual, her computer takes a long time to boot up. As it does, it makes all these weird noises and flashes error messages, which Mary is used to by now. She uses that time to plan her week, catch up on voicemails, and get herself a coffee. Some Mondays, her computer takes close to half an hour to boot up.

She could live with the slow boot-up time—after all, it's only once a week. But the computer's unreliability really gets on Mary's nerves. Some days her computer works like a charm. Other times, it is slow, unresponsive, and crashes for no good reason. This typically happens when she needs it most, for example, right before a meeting.

Mary has a nice nickname for her computer: "old piece of crap." Mary isn't an expert in computers by any means, but she can recognize a run-down computer when she sees one.

Mary is your typical home electronics consumer. She owns a tablet computer to check her social network and keep in touch with friends and family. Her son plays video games on a gigantic monster of a machine, and her daughter uses one of those slim, sleek laptops for her university work.

Mary is also the one who deals with her cable and Internet provider. She just updated her home connection and expected to have horrendous service, as we are used to when it comes to cable companies. Instead, she was pleased to see the technician arrive on time (no more "We'll be there between 8 and 5") and work efficiently.

She's by no means an expert, but she knows how to use her devices and manage her household. If she can keep her computers and Internet connection working, why can't IT do the same at work?

What 150,000 users told us

Mary is not the only one in her situation. In fact, our research showed that over 45 percent of users are dissatisfied with their computer. When we consider that office workers spend an average of 5.5 hours a day in front of a screen, this number is alarmingly high.

We compiled and analyzed the results of over 100,000 user-satisfaction surveys from our clients. The respondents came from all sorts of industries, company sizes, and user types. Because our clients tended to be more progressive, we recruited another 50,000 respondents from other organizations. We don't claim that these results are statistically representative or that they bear any kind of resemblance to your users. But they do provide useful insights on what drives satisfaction.

SATISFACTION

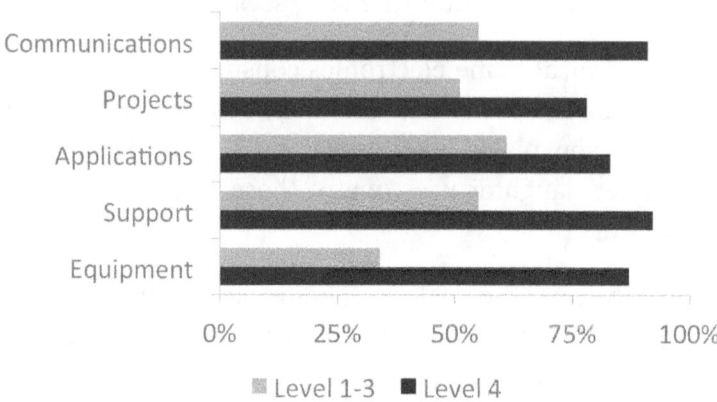

Level 1-3 Level 4

Of course, this is different for Level 4 IT departments. They consistently achieve high levels of user satisfaction in both Equipment (computers, cell phones, printers, etc.) and Support (help-desk, onsite support, application support, etc.).

Of all the different variables, none can predict business value as well as user satisfaction, to the point where we saw no organization's Level 4 IT department have a low level of user satisfaction.

Not all needs are equal

This correlation makes a lot of intuitive sense. After all, who would trust a partner if they cannot deliver basic services properly?

To illustrate the reason behind this, let me take you back a few years to your psychology classes. Perhaps you remember Maslow's Hierarchy of Needs. Maslow developed a pyramid of human needs that are layered in the order they should be achieved.

MASLOW HIERARCHY OF NEEDS

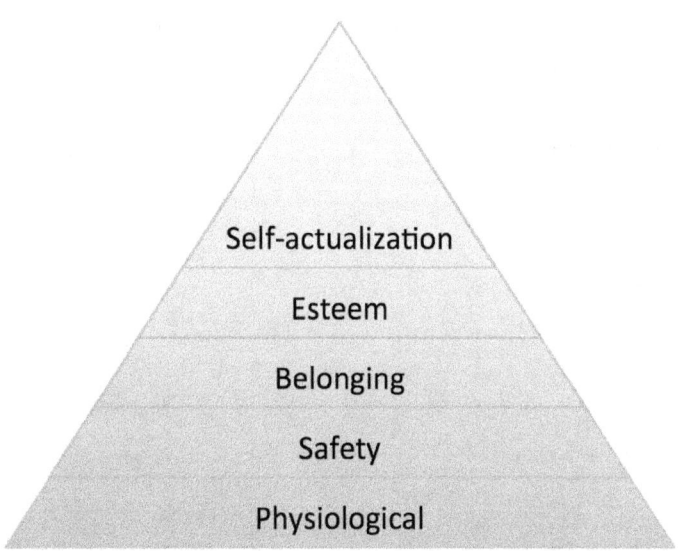

This pyramid suggests that individuals cannot fulfill their higher-order needs (such as self-esteem) if their lower-level needs aren't first met.

If my house just burned down, I won't be interested in joining a bowling league to meet my belonging needs. I am still working on my physiological needs. Later on, when I have appropriate shelter, I might become interested.

This pyramid is important because it shows how people's priorities vary based on whether they feel their basic needs are being met. And because it is subjective, someone with $5 in their bank account might feel rich and move on to their belonging needs, while someone else might feel terror and must further work on their security needs.

The same concept applies in IT. We call it the *IT Value Hierarchy*.

IT Value Hierarchy: Maslow applied to IT

The IT Value Hierarchy is built alongside Maslow's Hierarchy of Needs. It provides an overview of an organization's needs in their order of importance.

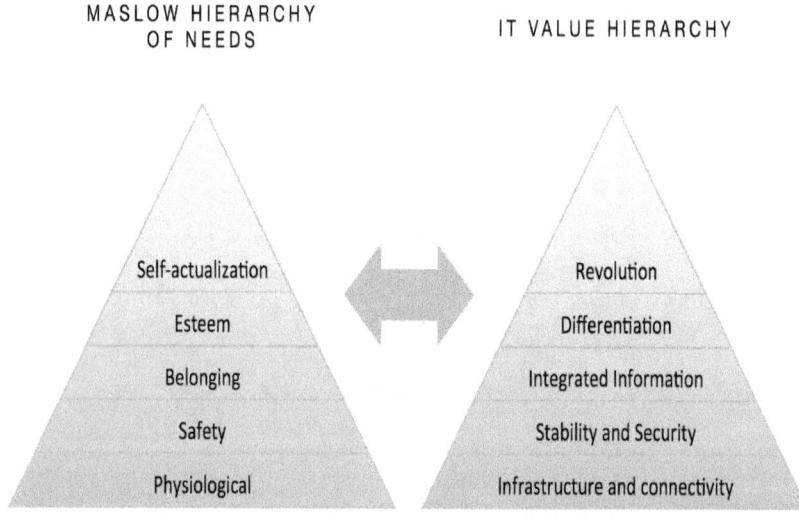

IT leaders tend to look at the third level (integrated information) and the fourth level (differentiation) when they talk about the business value of IT. They think of applications and the ways in which IT can enable the business to do more. But users won't be able to recognize the value in these propositions if they don't feel that their basic needs are being met. What are their basic needs? The thing they spend 5.5 hours a day sitting in front of: their computer.

Intuitively, it makes a lot of sense. Users frustrated by a slow computer won't care if you give them more data. They have a hard enough time using what they have that they won't bother with anything else.

> ### How Level 4 delivers the Basics
>
> Level 4 IT departments deliver the Basics in three ways:
>
> 1. They provide reliable infrastructure.
> 2. They treat user support as their core business.
> 3. They personalize their services for each user.
> 4. They measure satisfaction.

1. Reliable infrastructure

"My computer takes thirty minutes to boot up every Monday morning."

"My system crashes at least twice a day."

"My computer regularly disconnects from the network."

These are actual comments from users responding to our user-satisfaction survey.

Some years ago, while doing a client presentation, my computer decided to perform a virus scan. Corporate IT had decided that all computers would get scanned at noon every Wednesday, whether you wanted them to or not. This process brought my computer to a crawl, making the presentation almost impossible. This is particularly annoying when you work for Gartner and charge your clients a small fortune for giving IT advice.

Nothing is more frustrating than an unreliable piece of equipment. Imagine if your car decided to stop at any time while you were driving. After a few times, you would simply replace the car. There is no sense in owning a car if you cannot depend on it.

Most users don't report reliability issues. Like everything else, they always think it can wait for a different day. They are too busy right now. So, they live with the problem, their frustration increasing all the time, until the day they finally get fed up or the equipment gives out altogether.

The impact of poor performance

Computers are at the first level of the IT value hierarchy. If a computer doesn't work, nothing else matters.

But poor performance is not just annoying. Researchers have shown that computer malfunctions have a dramatic impact on user's task performance.

Test subjects were asked to do simple tasks on a computer in the psychology lab. But, of course, the evil scientists had rigged the computer so that it would simulate a malfunction at random intervals. The test subjects would go and try to do their tasks, but the computer would signal a problem, slow down, or reboot. The test subjects were asked to keep going despite the computer problems.

A similar group performed the same task without the constant issues. The results were dramatic. The non-annoyed group showed, on average, a success rate of 97 percent, while the annoyed group completed only 74 percent of the task.

The interesting part of this research was not only the performance, but the stress and anxiety it created within the test subjects.

Subjects in the annoyed group reported three times more stress on their self-evaluation than the non-annoyed group. They were also much less likely to help out with a second task and generally were less courteous with the researchers. The poor performance had real impacts on the well-being of the test subjects.

Now imagine if your computer was unreliable—all the time?

High-value organization users report, on average, a 3 to 4 percent complaint rate on their equipment's performance. Low-value organizations tend to report a 15 to 20 percent rate of complaints on computer performance—and these are only the ones that bother complaining.

The machine is the main representation of IT

Most users have no idea what it takes to manage an IT organization. They've never seen a server room—or a server, for that matter. They don't realize the kilometers of cabling required to provide access to the Internet, the complexity of keeping it all working together, or the costs involved. The only thing users see is their computer.

For the users, IT *is* their computer

They will judge the IT organization based on how well their computer is working. Poor computer performance typically means that IT is not doing its job.

Level 4 IT departments realize that their reputation depends on the users' computers and act accordingly. They work hard to minimize annoyances.

The real cost of performance

Many users face poor computer performance on a daily basis. Slow computers frustrate workers everywhere, especially when they have a better computer at home.

We performed an analysis for a client dealing with a major issue of slow computers. We calculated that, on average, they spent $15,000 per year per user on IT. Their current computer equipment cost $600 per user. Because computers have a lifespan of four years, computer costs amounted to $150 per year, or 1 percent of the IT budget.

As we mentioned, users spend an average of 5.5 hours per day in front of the computer, which is the most visible representation of the

IT organization. Yet, this client spent only 1 percent of their budget on computers.

We made a radical hypothesis: What if we doubled the amount of money they spent on computers? What would happen?

We bought a few machines and provided them to different users, with amazing results. Performance improved, productivity increased (according to the users), and users were much happier. The client decided to go ahead with the program.

This decision had an impact of 1 percent on their IT budget. Yet, satisfaction tripled. There is a big difference between a $600 and a $1,200 computer. Yet, given their budget, it was almost insignificant. They were able to absorb it without consequences.

So, why won't most IT departments spend more on computers? Two reasons:

- **The Best Buy Effect**: Most executives get the Best Buy flyer at home, and they use it to compare IT costs. When they see that they can get a decent computer for $500, they question IT on why they are spending so much on equipment.

- **It's one of the few costs IT managers can control**. Most IT costs are fixed (salaries, licenses, etc.). If IT managers want to reduce costs, IT leaders have few ways to do it. Cutting equipment may be one of the only available options.

Cutting equipment cost provides short-term relief but ends up costing a lot more in the long term.

Equipment is the easy part

For most IT departments, providing performant, reliable equipment is the easy part. After all, it is mainly money. There is no inherent complexity in providing a performing infrastructure. IT departments with an evergreening process will be able to master this part easily.

Yet, as the survey has shown, it is still one of the biggest issues IT leaders face.

2. Support as their core business

Some IT departments see user support as a necessary evil, a cost to reduce and manage. If only users would stop calling!

And this attitude shows in the way they manage it. They hire the cheapest technicians they can find. They understaff the help-desk. They give little to no authority to their technicians to make decisions on the go. And the help-desk manager often has so many tasks to juggle that he or she cannot spend time actually managing.

Most help-desks are in a pitiful state.

But that's not the case with Level 4 IT departments. For them, support is their core business. Let's see how they do this.

Ease of interaction

"I will need you to open a ticket before I can look into this problem."

There is no better way to make the user feel like a number. What it says is, "You might be facing a crisis, but our processes are more important. And don't count on me to do your job for you."

When users call the help-desk, their level of anxiety is already high. They are trying to perform a task, maybe even facing a deadline, and their computer won't cooperate. They've tried a few solutions already, without success. They are not happy campers. And then, just when they decide to give up and call for help, they are rewarded with more nonsense.

The thing users hate the most is the infamous ticketing system. They feel it is an obstacle to getting help. They resent having to both fill out a form and call for help.

But, of course, no IT organization can function without a ticketing system. It helps track, coordinate, and manage the resolution of requests. The issue is not with the system, but how IT uses it.

Level 4 IT departments make ample use of the ticketing system, but they don't let it get in the way of good service. For example, agents on the phone will open the tickets themselves on behalf of the client instead of asking them to do it. They will simplify the request form so that it includes only the most important information. And they don't close a ticket until they receive confirmation from the user that the problem has been solved.

Hours of operation

I had just started as CIO and was reviewing the different processes—and, of course, there were quite a few of them.

But then, I reviewed the system to submit problems to the help-desk. Of course there was no phone number—all tickets had to be sent through the website. And, if that was not enough of an irritant, the help-desk operated only between 8:30 a.m. and 4:30 p.m. This might make sense when dealing with office workers, but we were supporting twenty-two plants that operated twenty-four hours a day, seven days a week.

The team's response to my inquiry was that someone was always on call via pager for critical issues. But, if someone called for a simple problem, they were turned away.

The team could hardly have made it clearer that it just didn't want the plants to call. A big *Go Away* sign would not have been any more efficient.

Supporting the users

Next to the computer equipment, users interact with IT through the help-desk. In fact, users contact the help-desk once per month on average.

But the help-desk is not the easiest place to develop a good reputation. After all, users call only when they have a problem and may already be in a high state of anxiety, stress, or even panic. All they want is to resolve the problem as quickly as possible, so they can get back to whatever they were doing. The help-desk provides a good opportunity for any IT department to make mortal enemies (almost).

Through our studies, we have identified the principal dimensions by which users judge the help-desk:

- Ease of interaction

- Competencies

- Quality

Competencies

A few years ago, my wife and I went shopping for orthodontists for our daughter. Attempting to be good parents, we decided to visit at least three orthodontists and try to pick the best one.

So, we asked our friends to recommend their orthodontists and scheduled appointments. We talked about our criteria, what was important to us, and what we were looking to get out of the treatment. We spent what felt like days discussing and visiting dentist offices, but we quickly came to a realization:

I had no way to distinguish a good dentist from a really good dentist.

I just don't know enough about teeth to make that assessment. For me, they are all the same. Of course I can spot a bad dentist. He or she will be hesitant or will answer questions in a confusing manner, etc. But everything above "average" is all the same for me.

In the end, we chose one that inspired trust. He talked us through the procedure, was nice and friendly, and took his time. So, in the end, we chose the dentist based on his good customer service, not his technical skills.

The same holds true for users. Most of them know little about IT. They might have a computer at home and be able to do the most basic of debugging, but that's about it.

But what users *are* good at recognizing is bad customer service. Any technician who doesn't take the time to listen to the problem, or who is abrupt or shows contempt, will always be noticed. In fact, customer service skills are twice as important as technical skills.

High-value organizations spend an average of eight hours per year training their technicians on customer service skills. Phone etiquette, issue resolution, stress management—all the tools technicians need to successfully interact with users. Managers also listen in on calls and review emails to provide coaching to the technicians. For them, customer service is a not only a priority but a daily preoccupation.

Quality

How many users complain when a problem is not resolved to their satisfaction? According to our research, less than 5 percent. Users will call the help-desk again only if the problem prevents them from doing their work. But we know that, in IT, one problem might hide a second and third problem. How do we make sure that users call us back?

High-value departments don't wait for the phone call—they make the call.

When a problem is non-routine, they make a point of calling the user back a day or two later to make sure the problem is still resolved. This helps address any issues proactively, but it also shows the user that the IT department cares about their problems; that they are not just a number or a ticket to close.

An opportunity to shine, or to fail

It takes seven positive interactions to erase a negative one. With approximately twelve contacts per year, the help-desk cannot fail too often.

High-value IT departments insist that every single interaction with the user be positive. This doesn't mean that they bend over backward to meet users' needs. That would be unrealistic. But it does mean that they treat each interaction with courtesy and respect—respect for the user and their time.

They also realize that all this doesn't happen by accident. It requires a high level of effort. Processes are documented, metrics are in place, and a manager is accountable and coaches the team in the right direction. Level 4 IT departments actively manage the service.

3. Service personalization

IT departments reduce cost through standardization. The fewer types of computers, equipment, and software needed, the less they cost to purchase and maintain. In fact, if everyone had the same equipment, it would make everything much simpler.

But the reality is different. Not everyone is similar or has the same needs. Trying to push a standard solution on everyone leaves everyone dissatisfied. Someone on the road will want a light, easy-to-carry computer whereas an Excel-jockey will beg for a bigger screen.

Level 4 IT departments have found a way to meet specific user needs without losing sight of standardization. They acknowledge that not everyone can be served with the "Desktop or laptop?" way of looking at the world. This is why they've developed user profiles, or personas.

Personas represent the needs of a particular segment of the population. They share the same needs and can thus be accommodated with the same type of equipment and services.

Personas are based on users' needs, not their position or status. Thus, two salespersons might have the same title but be in different personas.

Every organization has different personas, but the following six are typical for a start:

- **Office workers**: The most standard IT users. Sit at their desks and use basic systems and productivity applications.

- **Power users**: Work with advanced or power-hungry applications (auto cad, video editing, etc.). Require a higher level of control over equipment. Also includes office workers who like to experiment with new applications.

- **Mobile workers**: Always on the road. Need quick access to their systems without breaking their backs.

- **Managers/professionals**: Their days are spent checking emails and running from one meeting to the next.

- **Executives**: Like business professionals but also include a lot of traveling. Work odd hours and weekends.

- **Occasional users**: Don't need a dedicated computer. Can use shared equipment, a mobile device, or a home computer.

The value of creating personas comes from developing solution sets to fit user needs. Each persona has a specific equipment model assigned to it and a specific configuration and image. IT departments go to great lengths to adapt each "kit" to their needs.

For example, one IT department went as far as preconfiguring the Starbucks Wi-Fi in their image for people on the road. After all, Starbucks is their second office.

This concept of personas allows the IT department to stay in touch with real user needs.

4. Satisfaction measurement

How do you know if you've delivered the Basics? Level 4 IT departments keep it simple: they ask the users.

IT's definition of delivering the Basics might differ from the user community. What you think is a fast computer might be inadequate for their everyday needs.

Asking the user is the only way to know if IT delivers the Basics. User satisfaction surveys are an easy and reliable way to measure the Basics.

Satisfaction is the difference between the service delivered and the service expected. If the service delivered exceeds user expectations, then the user will likely be satisfied. But, if the service delivered is lower than user expectations, the user will be dissatisfied.

Satisfaction measures the Basics

IT departments have always been good at managing and measuring the service part of satisfaction. They understand what it takes to deliver good service and try to improve their service offering over time. No one gets up in the morning to give a bad level of service.

Expectation, on the other hand, is difficult to measure. Satisfaction surveys provide an easy way to measure the expectations side of the equation and to change it over time.

Satisfaction as a performance metric

Level 4 IT departments not only measure satisfaction, they do it monthly. This allows them to treat satisfaction just like any other key performance indicator.

Of course, no user would want to be surveyed every month, which is why the IT departments use a different sample every month. Feedback is continual, without having to harass users.

Level 4 IT departments receive two main benefits from measuring satisfaction monthly:

Benefit 1. They better understand what drives satisfaction.

If you regularly measure satisfaction, you get more chances to understand what has an impact. For example the survey showed that the operating system update had a negative impact on user satisfaction. Then the team used that information to make changes, at which point satisfaction went back up. Later on, the desktop renewal project made a lasting positive impact on user satisfaction.

We can also see which variables have an impact on satisfaction: user location, type of equipment, age of equipment, and type of user. For example, if we see that a particular office has low satisfaction, it hints at performance issues specific to that location. This helps the IT department make decisions that are based on solid facts instead of on impressions.

Benefit 2. It motivates the team.

If I weigh myself in the morning, chances are I won't eat dessert (or at least not as much) at night. Simply having this regular feedback loop helps motivate people to stay on the right path.

Level 4 IT departments use satisfaction as a motivation tool to encourage their team. When satisfaction goes up, they look at what they've done that worked. When it goes down, they use this as a way to remind everyone of the importance of everyday behaviors.

Being project-focused means it is easy to lose track of the mundane tasks. Having a constant reminder helps to keep us on track.

A few myths on satisfaction

Users are impossible to please

"Users want everything! They are impossible to satisfy!"—*CIO of a manufacturing company*

It's tempting to think that users want everything and anything. After all, they are not the ones paying for the services.

But, in fact, we find that users tend to be very reasonable in their expectations. Most users simply want the tools they need to do their job. Very few users have disproportionate expectations. After all, they have experience working for different organizations and know what is realistic.

Satisfaction is expensive

One of the most common reasons to avoid focusing on satisfaction that I hear from IT leaders is that they lack the budget for it. "Of course, if you have an enormous IT budget, then it's easy to satisfy your users, but we're struggling to make ends meet!"

So, it begs the question: just how much does it cost to satisfy users?

One study compared IT budget with user satisfaction. It looked at different IT departments across industries and sizes. We would expect that the organizations with the lowest IT budgets would have very dissatisfied users, while those with huge budgets would have ecstatic users.

Instead, the study found no correlation between the budget and the level of satisfaction. It's impossible to predict the level of user satisfaction simply on the basis of budget alone.

I agree that it is easier to focus on satisfaction when you have the budget and staff available to help out. But a tight budget shouldn't be a reason not to try.

Users will always be dissatisfied

IT leaders commonly repeat the theme that there will always be users that are not happy. This phrase is like a mantra for some, used as a reply for every complaint against their services. "Someone complained in finance about the response time of the application." "Well, there will always be someone that is not happy."

Well, this may be true. After all, we cannot please everyone all the time. But we can please most of the people, most of the time.

Using this type of language becomes a way for IT leaders to accept dissatisfied users.

In fact, high-performing organizations have less than 1 percent of detractors. Satisfying almost everyone *is* possible.

I would know if users were unhappy

"We have an open culture—people aren't shy about complaining. I don't need to measure; they would tell me if they were not happy."

Are you happy with every single one of your suppliers? Did you complain to them? After all, you have a culture of openness. That's right, few people complain when they are dissatisfied.

Why don't users complain? There are three main reasons:

1. They don't know who to complain to. Unless you provide clear instructions for users to lodge a complaint, they don't know who to talk to. When asked, only 14 percent of users knew the name of the person in charge of IT.

What gets measured gets done.

2. They don't think it will change anything. Either they complained in the past (or someone close to them did) and nothing changed, or they don't believe in your ability to change.

3. They are afraid of retribution. They are concerned that they may suffer consequences if they complain (bad service, loss of support, etc.).

Retailers take complaints seriously because only 4 percent of dissatisfied customers complain. The others vote with their feet (shop at a different store) or complain to their friends and family instead. Because only one person in twenty tells them when there is an issue, they do their best to address it.

"But I'm not getting any complaints."

If you are not receiving complaints, it must mean that your service is great, right? Consider this: the top 5 percent of IT departments receive, on average, complaints from 3 percent of their users annually. Therefore, the real question to ask is: are you better than the top 5 percent of IT departments, or did your users give up?

Every communication from IT should include a link or a phone number for people to voice their concerns, with guaranteed anonymity.

Becoming Level 4: Providing the Basics

For users to be engaged, they must first not feel dissatisfied. If systems are slow, difficult to use, or unreliable, users will not rely on them to do their job. They will attempt the minimum required to get by. On the other hand, if the Basics are in place, users have a solid platform they can depend on. We're not going to cover how you can manage infrastructure. Chances are, you're very good at this already. What we will cover, instead, is how to make sure you meet everyone's needs.

Earlier, we learned that there is only one way to know if users are satisfied: ask. We can't rely on complaints (less than 4 percent of users complain) or on business leaders, as they often are not connected to that level of detail. No, to get good feedback on whether we are getting the Basics right, we need to run a user-satisfaction survey.

Once a year is not enough

Fifty percent of IT departments don't measure user satisfaction. What is the main reason for this? They are afraid that it will raise expectations: if users voice issues, they will expect resolutions. Additionally, IT departments feel it is unnecessary. Either they think the users are satisfied and measuring will not add any value, or they know the users are dissatisfied, so what's the point in putting it in numbers?

We've found both cases to be wrong. IT leaders are poor judges of user satisfaction. They either spend too much time resolving issues and thus think everyone is dissatisfied, or they are disconnected from operational realities and think everyone is satisfied. The reality is often more in the middle.

The other 50 percent typically measure satisfaction on a yearly basis. One month before the survey, everyone cleans up their act in order to look good. They fix computers, clear the support ticket backlog, and install new equipment, doing their best to get the numbers up. For about a month after the survey, they spend their time pointing out everything that could explain the poor results or taking the merit for any increase. And then, they finally forget about satisfaction for another ten months, until everything starts all over again.

Once a year is not enough. We've found that users evaluate the last six weeks when they respond to user satisfaction surveys. Anything before that is too hazy. Users have a very short-term appreciation of IT services, so although your yearly survey might show good results, they might not be valid in another six weeks.

Level 4 IT departments measure satisfaction monthly—and they do not measure only post-ticket satisfaction from the last interaction.

They send an actual user-satisfaction survey to measure every aspect of IT services every single month. But, of course, users would get fed up if they received a survey every month, which is why the IT department uses a statistical sampling method to send the survey to only a portion of users every month. No user receives a survey more than once or twice a year. This method provides constant feedback without annoying anyone.

Gone in ninety seconds

One of the problems with surveys is that users lie. And not because they are mean—nothing like that—because they are bored. Most surveys are too long and ask questions that are not relevant. People get tired of answering surveys after ninety seconds. We've seen that the time it takes to respond to a survey question reduces significantly after ninety seconds, to the point where we doubt people even had time to read the question, let alone give it serious thought.

We have ninety seconds to get to the crux of the matter with users. And yet, most surveys spend the first ninety seconds asking for demographic data ("What business unit are you in?", "What role are you?"). This is a waste of good feedback. To be effective, your survey should start with the important questions first, before the users have time to lose interest.

Anonymity

The second reason users lie is because the survey is not anonymous. People are afraid to either get in trouble or to create trouble for someone in IT. When we run surveys for our clients, we guarantee anonymity to the users. The IT department will never be able to access the data about specific user responses. This helps quite a bit in getting good responses. Users simply know that they can be honest without any consequences. But what if you run the survey yourself?

In that case, be very clear about who will have access to the data and who will not. Reassure the user that no one in IT will see his or her individual responses. And then live by it. It is tempting to try to match names with comments or ratings. Don't. The word will get out, and your future surveys will be useless.

The "Quickest Survey Ever"

Too often, surveys try to include diagnostic data in order to pinpoint problems. Of course, these questions are useful only if you've been able to think of all the various potential problems that can arise. And it makes no sense to show them to users who don't think a problem exists in the first place.

A fifteen-minute survey that tries to cover all possible scenarios will only end up wasting the user's and your own time. Why? Users are notoriously bad at diagnosing problems. A user finds his or her computer slow. Is it because of the personal computer? Because of all the malware installed by mistake? Because of the internal network, the link to the Internet? Or because of the performance of the application used most frequently? Users are typically unable to make the distinction.

User surveys serve to highlight that a problem exists. Aside from this, they have little diagnostic utility. It is better to use the warning flags and combine them with analyses to fix the real problems.

Here is an example of the simplest survey you can use and get amazing feedback:

Overall, how satisfied are you with IT services?

(1 = very dissatisfied, 7 = very satisfied)

1   2   3   4   5   6   ⦿ 7

How satisfied are you with the following:

(1 = very dissatisfied, 7 = very satisfied, NA - not applicable)

	NA	1	2	3	4	5	6	7
Equipment (computers, phones, mobiles, network, etc.)								⦿
Support (phone support, on-site support)								⦿
Applications (support, maintenance, evolution)								⦿
Projects								⦿
Communications from IT (messages, notifications, etc)								⦿

This is the starting point of the survey we use with our clients. The survey is very simple and takes only seconds to fill out, providing two advantages: people will gladly complete it, and the responses will be meaningful (with no survey fatigue).

Analyzing the results

The "Quickest Survey Ever" produces a surprisingly long analysis report. The reason: we already know quite a bit about our users. You don't have to ask your users which business unit they are from—you already know that. You don't have to ask them what kind of equipment they have, where they are located, or how often they call the help-desk. This information is already available to you. But, of course, this does require tracking the responses, thus the need for confidentiality.

This survey allows us to compare satisfaction against several different dimensions. Some of the most interesting dimensions we've seen are:

Department: That's an obvious and necessary one that will be used in the partnership plan later on, but it also shows how business units vary in their use and expectations of IT services.

Geography: Different offices, localities, or cities/countries can highlight problems specific to one area.

Years of service: This is also an interesting dimension. For example, new employees with a low score often show a deficient onboarding. Dissatisfaction with employees at three to four years of service often shows equipment near the end of its life. Speeding up the evergreening process can produce rapid results to increase satisfaction.

Number of tickets per month: Are people who regularly call the help-desk more or less satisfied with IT?

User persona: If you've tagged each user with a persona, then it is interesting to see the satisfaction associated with each persona. Are your standards adequate?

Equipment: What type of equipment do the users have? Are people happier with laptops or desktops? Is the new model of computer better than the last one?

Satisfaction metrics as the drivers of change

The satisfaction survey results can then help us make plans to improve the situation. It is tempting to make a big list of issues and try to work through them all at once. This is an easy way to make everyone hate this program. And, unsurprisingly, it doesn't work all that well. Several of the issues are dependent on one another or have common causes. We've found it is best to focus on two to three issues per month. This gives a manageable workload to the support or infrastructure team and allows it to see continual progress over time. It puts everyone in an incremental-improvement mindset.

It also creates a scientific-management mindset. Where we typically had a problem, found a solution, and called it good, we now retest to see if the problem is actually resolved. Survey data comes in every month, so it is easy to see the real impact of an action plan. Teams can follow a systematic process to diagnose the problem, develop a hypothesis as to the cause, perform actions to fix the problem, and use the next month's survey to confirm the hypothesis. Is satisfaction better? Then the hypothesis was probably the right one. Is it stable or down? Then the hypothesis was false, and it is time to go back to the drawing board.

Diagnostics -> Hypothesis -> Action items - > Measure

Below, you'll see an actual plan graciously shared by one of my clients to serve as an example:

Issue	Action items	Results
Albany office has lower equipment satisfaction	Investigate if it is networking issue	March: Worked with telco supplier to resolve issue. April: Satisfaction back to normal
Mobile professionals persona dissatisfied with CRM performance	Work with cell provider to investigate coverage and speed issues	May: No difference in satisfaction
	Work with application team to investigate mobile settings	June: Slight improvement in satisfaction
	Follow user in the field to understand usage pattern. Found nonoptimal use of the tools. Retrain users.	July: Found nonoptimal use of the tools. Retrained affected users. August: Satisfaction back in line

In the previous example, we see that the user-satisfaction survey pointed out a network-performance issue in one of the satellite offices, something that stayed below the radar as an irritant that no one had actually contacted support about. We also see that the sales force suffered from slow CRM performance on their mobile devices. After some experimentation, they saw that it wasn't a system problem but a usage problem. IT retrained the users (through an email and a two-minute video), and the problem disappeared.

See it in action

See the survey in action and an example of analysis at:

GreenElephantTeam.com/BVIT

Removing obstacles

We already talked about the consequence of poor equipment performance on stress and the perception of value. Intuitively, we all agree that, if using the system is slow and frustrating, the users will do the minimum required. They will certainly refuse to explore, experiment, and generally play around in the system.

The problem with dissatisfiers is that they quickly become invisible. My daughter attends an international baccalaureate school. As such, they promote openness to the world by teaching about other cultures and languages. To demonstrate this, they hung six different clocks over the reception area, each showing a different city in a different time zone. The concept is great—except that none of the clocks work. It seems their batteries ran out some time ago. How long ago? Well, at least six years. I first noticed them when my daughter started kindergarten. Six years later, they still don't work.

When we spend all our time in one place, these things become invisible. But, when you are new, they are flagrant. If you have ever had buyers visiting your house while it is up for sale, you probably noticed all the small problems that were previously invisible. The spot on the ceiling. The missing drawer handle. Barely noticeable before, such flaws now appear to glow in the dark.

Finding dissatisfiers often takes a fresh set of eyes. It is difficult to do this when sitting alone in our office.

Strategies for finding dissatisfiers:

- Ask the users: They probably live with several little annoyances that are not worth their time to call in to the help-desk.
- Ask new hires: Everything is new. Small issues are probably very obvious to them.
- Use the common areas: Use the departmental printers, conference rooms, and Wi-Fi access throughout the different business units.
- Keep a list: Record the dissatisfiers as they are identified and fixed. This list can be used to better plan future initiatives and also to track progress over time.

What are your dissatisfiers?

But, of course, the computer represents only the tip of the iceberg, so to speak. IT depends on countless infrastructure: servers, networks, applications, databases, etc. All need to work in order for the "computer" to work. Being in control of the infrastructure is a prerequisite to business value. IT departments that lack the minimum stability and performance will not be able to provide an adequate user experience. Besides computer performance, what are the top dissatisfiers that impact users everywhere? We analyzed the survey data and found five recurring themes that affect satisfaction.

Installing applications

IT departments tend to lock computers, preventing users from installing new applications. The reason is simple: it helps keep computers secure, reducing the number of issues and, thus, the number of calls to the help-desk. But it also does something else: it handcuffs the users.

Several free or cheap tools and services exist that can help a user's life, but the process required to request access to these tools is so difficult that most users prefer to do without.

Instead, they start using web-based applications, without IT's knowledge.

The departmental printer

"How hard can it be to simply change the toner?"

We often hear IT technicians complain that users don't change the toner in the printers. The boxes are right there; it takes only a couple of minutes. Why don't they do it? And my response is always the same: "Did you make a fresh pot of coffee this morning?"

The problem with common assets, such as printers and coffee machines, is that no one feels like they are the owner. It's always someone else's problem. After all, we can always live without coffee. And our document can wait a few hours, at least until someone else changes the toner.

But someone must always do the work—someone that needs their copies right away for an important meeting and needs to change the toner, at the risk of ruining their white suit. And, of course, these people end up changing an unfair amount of toner cartridges compared to the others.

Is it IT's responsibility to change the toner? Why not? If it's an easy task for users, why shouldn't it be easy for IT as well? Most printers call home when toner is low. Integrating this into the help-desk routine would allow technicians to schedule toner-change runs. While they are there, they can inspect the equipment and make sure it is clean, working properly, and doing its job.

The conference room

Of course, the most frustrating part of using a conference room nowadays is simply finding one to begin with. It seems conference rooms are becoming very hard to come by. But finding one is only the first step.

The most entertaining part of meetings is the presenter trying to project his or her presentation. More often than not, the cable is too short, leaving only one possible seat that can be used. Then there's the adapter itself: good old VGA or HDMI? And the classic: will the projector recognize the computer on the first try? And it gets even better when we use so-called "intelligent equipment." The electronic whiteboard becomes more of a nightmare than a real help.

We didn't even talk about obtaining access to the network for people from outside the organization. Some companies still need a call to the help-desk—not practical when ten persons are waiting for the meeting to start.

And have you ever had to get on your knees under the table while wearing your most expensive business attire to find a power outlet?

What if we designed conference rooms with usability in mind? We tried it out, starting with longer cables. We set up longer VGA cables that could reach all around the room, allowing anyone in the room to present. The cost: minimal. Then we set up electrical outlets throughout the table, allowing people to connect their power supplies without crawling on the ground. We also wrote the guest Wi-Fi name under the projector screen, allowing guests to connect to the Internet without having to call anybody. We hung a poster with instructions on how to set up the projector. Although these instructions are rarely required, they allow people to troubleshoot the two to three most frequent issues by themselves. And, finally, we included the help-desk number so that anyone (including visitors) could call to report a problem before or during the meeting.

We also established a weekly check-up process. Every week a technician went around the conference rooms and made sure that cables worked, videoconference systems connected, and that everything was in order. This was necessary because most users don't call the help-desk when conference room equipment fails to work. They will move on to the next one or go without. The weekly check-up also made sure that consumables, such as dry-erase pens, pads of paper, etc., were replenished.

E-mail attachments

People live in their e-mails. Sharing files and such is a common occurrence for most professionals. But several e-mail systems still limit the size of attachments and the size of the mailbox. Why is that?

The IT department is usually concerned about the cost. How much will it cost if we have to open up storage for everyone? What would be the consequence?

Well, not that much.

Storage is cheap, and most e-mail providers provide high levels of disk space for ridiculous prices. Why can't users receive storage at work that is at least equivalent to what they get free from Google?

Providing "unlimited" storage is way cheaper than playing police.

Sharing with the outside world

Most IT departments have made it easy to share information internally. Document-management and collaboration tools are commonplace. But few business units share information with other business units. Instead, they share information with suppliers and clients.

A CIO received a call from Dropbox, the file-sharing company. The Dropbox representative informed the CIO that his company had over 150 paying customers. The CIO's users would save significantly if they were to choose a corporate plan instead. Of course the CIO was shocked! One hundred and fifty paying users! He wasn't aware that anyone used the service.

The reality is that a lot of business units need to share big documents with the outside world. Marketing needs to share advertising collateral with agencies. Legal needs to share contracts and documents. Engineering needs to share plans and CAD drawings with design firms. Most organizations aren't well-equipped to provide these tools.

Although I understand that security might limit your options, stopping access without offering alternatives is a good way to encourage users to bypass the system.

Users are not dissatisfied. We now know that they are in a good position to be engaged. But satisfaction is not engagement. Having people satisfied with your services and having them actively engaged are different stories altogether. Let's find out how to create engagement.

2. Engage the users

IT as a monopoly

"IT is a monopoly. Why should we care what users think?"

This meeting had a rough start. I had been invited to talk to an industry group of IT leaders about IT's role in organizations. We were in a nice hotel in a remote little town. The agenda was simple: how can IT departments play a strategic role within their organizations? We spent the morning discussing how no one in the room was sitting at the executive table. They were always being relegated to a sideline role. The IT leaders were frustrated by their lack of resources and credibility and felt they could contribute much more—but no one in the business was letting them. They had to fight just to maintain their infrastructure in semi-decent shape.

I explained the business value equation and met a lot of resistance. They argued that the remedy to their IT issues was not satisfying users, but instead getting more authority. They stayed focused on trying to identify ways IT could gain that legitimate authority through titles or standards (security and architecture).

After listening for a few hours, I suggested that they could achieve that legitimacy by demonstrating their contribution instead. I started talking about the role of user satisfaction in credibility, but I failed at it. They remained convinced that users didn't matter. We stopped for lunch, and everyone went their own ways to catch up on calls and e-mails.

After returning from lunch, I asked the key question: "Who's the real client of IT?"

Everyone started saying that the client is the one who pays for the service, that is, the president/CEO and the executives. "Fair enough," I said. "Now how many times have you changed 'clients' in the last few years?" Everyone started laughing. The executive suite seems to be a revolving door in most organizations. I then asked, "How many of these 'clients' used to be your 'users' before?" The laughing stopped.

I made the point that executives tend to be short-sighted. They look at optimizing costs or increasing revenues in the short term. But your users will be with you for years to come, perhaps even becoming your clients. Neglecting users, even if the "client" thinks it's okay, comes at a high price down the line: your credibility.

And that's when a lot of the IT leaders understood that they lacked credibility TODAY. They let their "clients" dictate the agenda. If they had treated their users differently a few years earlier, perhaps they would be at the executive table today. The meeting went much more smoothly afterward.

Engaging the users

IT has traditionally been in an economy mindset. Contrary to commercial organizations, IT doesn't get any benefits from "selling" more or from having users use more of its resources. The fewer resources users use, the easier it is to do everything within the budget.

IT has always thought that "if the business asks for it, then it's the business's problem if users do or don't use it." And, to some extent, they are right. After all, different business units bear responsibility for managing their employees, and if someone doesn't use the systems correctly, they must correct the situation.

But the reality has been different. Business units don't have the tools/time/knowledge to make certain their employees are using the systems properly. They don't know if the data are accurate, if the employees follow the process to the letter, or, better yet, if the employees use the system at all.

Old transactional applications were easy to monitor. If an employee didn't enter a sales order, then a product wouldn't get shipped. The process broke, making it easier to go back and identify the culprit.

But new applications derive their value not from transactions, but from their collaborative and analytical capabilities. In these cases, it is not clear if users are using the system or not.

I was talking one day with the head of the business intelligence business unit for a retail organization. He told me that only about 15 percent of the people who should use his system actually did. Everyone else was taking the bare minimum out of it, losing out on massive opportunities to optimize merchandising choices, pricing, and promotion decisions.

Level 4 IT departments do not wait for the business units or for the users to maximize their systems. They do it themselves. They focus on user engagement.

Define user engagement

The easiest definition of user engagement is the following: if the users were not obligated, would they still use your systems?

Engaged users see the value the systems provide to them on a day-to-day basis. They get value either through increased productivity, ease of collaboration, or new information that enables them to make decisions. The systems aren't there simply to follow a transactional process—they are there to help users reach their objectives and make users' lives easier.

But there are prerequisites to user engagement: the Basics must be in place first. As we saw in the last chapter, slow or unreliable computers will incite users to do the bare minimum. They'll avoid any unnecessary frustration. Still, having satisfied users doesn't mean we have engaged users.

How Level 4 IT departments engage users

Level 4 IT departments engage users in three ways:

- They train the users.
- They communicate with the users.
- They measure engagement.

1. Training the users

Back when I was a CIO, we deployed a new enterprise resource planning (ERP) across the organization, to employees with an average of twenty-plus years of service. Getting them to change and adopt new business practices was difficult at best.

One of the challenges we faced was getting people to show up and be attentive during the training sessions. Because the system was a few weeks away from being deployed, people didn't feel a sense of urgency. They thought it would be like what they had used in the past. And, of course, they were wrong.

To entice people to get trained, we developed a certification program. Each major process had a certification track with four levels:

Basic, Bronze, Silver, and Gold. The Basic was the bare minimum required to access the system. We went as far as preventing people from getting a user ID if they didn't pass the Basic certification. But the test was easy and only encouraged people to keep going.

Once they passed their test, they were given a framed diploma with a seal. Some of these people had never made it past high school. Others hadn't been to school in over twenty years. It was the only diploma they had received in recent years. Most of them hung it in their cubicles.

This certification process helped the users get engaged with training. Now they had an objective (a diploma) and a penalty (no access to the system) if they didn't go ahead with the process. It also gave them an evolution step (Bronze, Silver, and Gold) to learn and showcase their skills.

Of course, managing this program cost money. It required developing the certifications, tests, administration, and materials (diplomas, frames, etc.). But we figured we got a return on investment (ROI) within two months simply by analyzing the number of questions and calls coming in to the help-desk. People with a higher certification tended to have much fewer calls. Even more, the training acted as reference points, with people's qualifications visible from everyone else's cubicle.

Training roadmap

Most projects focus on training the users at the go-live stage. Do they have the skills required to use the system effectively at the time the system deploys? And then, the training stops, the project team is dismantled, and training becomes the responsibility of overworked super-users. Or worse, it falls to the wayside.

Thinking that you can provide enough training on day one to last a lifetime is overly optimistic. Most users begin by doing the bare minimum with their new system, trying to get their bearings after such a dramatic change. Then, as they grow more comfortable, they will start exploring to see how the system can become easier to use or make them more productive. And, later on, they will see what else the system can do for them and what features they simply didn't know existed.

But, too often, users stay at the first stage. They lack the access, the skill, or the knowledge to further expand the use of their systems.

Level 4 IT departments don't leave the users to themselves in that process. They develop training roadmaps with levels of evolution not only to inform users that there is more to the system than what they are doing right now, but also to motivate users to reach these levels.

The training roadmaps can be well-defined with certification gates (as we've seen in our example) or informal, managed by a series of training classes or workshops. Either way, it helps users understand that they can be more productive or better informed than they are right now. It also gives them time to acclimate themselves with the system instead of getting shown everything all at once.

Training takes many forms

Level 4 IT departments provide training in many forms:

- Formal classroom training: useful for new system deployment.
- Clips/videos: useful for "how-to" and providing refresher training.
- Lunch-and-learn: good for showcasing helpful functionalities.
- Help-desk: used to provide rapid, just-in-time training.

But providing training can quickly become costly. This is why Level 4 IT departments let the users themselves help out. Knowledgeable users can easily train other users, through lunch-and-learns, for example.

Taking ownership

Training can be the responsibility of different groups within the organization. Sometimes, human resources has all the training budget and resources, while at other times, it is the business units themselves. Level 4 IT departments take an ownership role regardless of who is really responsible.

They understand that the users need appropriate and ongoing training to make the most of their systems. Without training, the users will simply revert back to being passive and unengaged.

2. Communication with the users

It's easy to think we are good communicators. After all, we send messages to the users and listen to their complaints. So, why does it seem like a complete and total waste of time? Why do we get the feeling that users are simply not interested in hearing from us?

What we take for indifference is often simply a failure to communicate properly. A relationship requires constant communication to stay in the front of the mind. Without communication, it is easy to be forgotten.

Level 4 organizations have at least three interactions per month with each user. What's an interaction? It can be any of the following:

- Call to the help-desk
- Follow-up to a previous request
- E-mail/announcement from IT
- Satisfaction survey
- Training capsule
- Etc.

But simply communicating is not enough. The communication needs to be planned, on-message, and relevant.

Boring

"I don't see the point. We keep sending e-mails, but no one reads them!"

I often hear that argument when I ask why IT doesn't communicate more with its users. They make it seem that users don't want to hear from IT. Yet, when we run IT satisfaction surveys, we see that 78 percent of users want to hear MORE often from IT, not less.

In fact, communication is a major cause of dissatisfaction. Users want to know what's happening, what's coming up, and how they can be better users. They want to get trained, following their own time constraints. And, most importantly, they want to know that IT is working for them.

Still, no one wants to stop and read the current communications from IT. They are simply too boring. Most IT communications have a level of formalism that is way too high, with an unclear message that is diluted in a lot of text.

We analyzed over two hundred e-mails sent from IT and identified five key problems with them:

Relevance

"The ERP system will not be available from 12:00 a.m. to 8:00 a.m. on Sunday." Great. That's important information for an ERP user, but I don't need to see this if I am not an ERP user. It only clutters my inbox and makes me want to dismiss the next e-mail from IT.

Laziness has prevented IT from building targeted mailing lists. Doing so saves a few minutes of work and has an impact on the relevance of your messages for years to come.

Frequency

How many communications are too many? If communications aren't relevant, then any communication is too many. But assuming they are relevant to the user, one to two communications a week are well received.

That sounds like a lot? It is. We're talking about eight communications a month. How many do you do today? If it's fewer than eight a month, users are forgetting about you.

Length

The average length of both Level 4 department communications and the other departments' communications is almost identical. Both tend to contain approximately two hundred words. The main difference is that we can typically stop reading Level 4 messages after twenty words. Everything necessary to understand the communication is in the beginning of the message. Everything else simply provides more background information to anyone that might be interested. But, by simply reading the first couple of lines, the user knows exactly what the communication is about.

Focus

How many topics are part of the message? More than one constitutes a problem. The most successful messages address only one topic at a time. Two things to talk about? Make it two distinct messages.

System down

One of the issues we faced was how to make our e-mail notifications more relevant. It seemed that most of the e-mails coming from IT started with the subject: "IT Notification:....." Although it clearly showed who it was from, this was already obvious from the sender, which was also called "IT Notification." The objective was to reduce the number of calls to the help-desk when a system was down. It is always a frustrating process when a system goes down. First, users think it's only them, so they play around trying to fix their computer, perhaps even rebooting it. Then they ask colleagues around them. Eventually, they call the help-desk, only to be put on hold due to an influx of calls. Finally, they are told that it is a system issue and that "we are working on it. We don't know when it will be resolved."

To make the process easier on everyone, we created a new e-mail notification account, called "System Status." Each notification consisted of two different subjects: "XYZ is down. We'll update you as we know more," and "XYZ is up! Thanks."

These two notifications were sent to the users as soon as a problem was suspected with a system. The users knew then that they could stop working on it and move on to something else until they got the go-ahead message. In the message itself, we had a big red thumbs down and a big green thumbs up. Without reading the message, it was very obvious was it was about.

But the key to our success was the segmentation of the list. Not everyone got the notifications—only the specific users of the system. We produced (and managed) a mailing list for each system to facilitate this communication.

The net result: users saw only those notifications that helped them, we reduced the number of calls to the help-desk when an event happened, and, more importantly, we reduced the frustration users experienced when dealing with system problems.

Feedback loop

Developing better messages is one thing. But is it working?

Talk to any marketer, and they will give you some sobering statistics. E-mail marketing campaigns are doing well when they achieve an open rate of 4 percent. That is, e-mail campaigns (not spam) focusing on people interested in their products and services get read by only one out of every twenty-five people they are sent to.

We get a tremendous amount of e-mail, and it is easy to get lost in the mass.

Most IT departments send an e-mail and simply assume it will be read. Once they press send, whether the user reads it is not IT's problem anymore. They've done their part of the work.

Level 4 IT departments aren't satisfied with this approach. This is why they actually take the time to measure whether the e-mails have been opened and read and if any action has been taken.

Some Level 4 IT departments even go as far as running experiments. They send a different e-mail to two groups and determine which one is more successful: a longer or shorter subject line, the use of specific words ("Urgent," "Mandatory," etc.), tone (casual vs. business), and so on. This allows them to see which formula works best for their audience.

It also allows them to improve the impact of their communications.

Many cheap and easy-to-use tools exist today to facilitate this. The only thing preventing IT departments from running such experiments is that they don't bother.

Multichannel

But what about communication channels? It seems we always focus on e-mail for corporate communications, but e-mail is the least-preferred means of communication for the younger generation.

Are you leveraging SMS/text messages, tweets, Facebook posts, etc.? The same message can be communicated across different platforms to reach users the way they like to be reached and are most likely to take action.

Level 4 IT departments aren't shy about leveraging social media to reach users where they spend their time.

3. Engagement measurement

Imagine this scenario. You're sitting at your computer trying to do your staff's performance evaluations using the human resource (HR) system, but you are going nowhere fast. You're struggling with the categories and the different scoring systems available. After an hour, you decide to give up and try again later.

In the meantime, you receive an e-mail from HR inviting you to a refresher fifteen-minute video tutorial. You remember receiving a similar e-mail a couple of weeks ago, but you thought you didn't need the refresher back then. Now, however, the idea doesn't sound so bad.

Of course, this invitation didn't happen by accident. The HR system contains several user-engagement metrics, one of which is the time it takes to perform an evaluation. HR evaluated that it takes an average of fifteen minutes to perform an evaluation. Rarely does it take more than thirty minutes. So, someone who spends an hour on the same evaluation is facing trouble. The system thus sends out an automatic e-mail with the link to the refresher tool. No pressure—simply a quick e-mail that offers a little bit of help.

This kind of user-engagement monitoring can make a significant difference to the user experience. Users might not realize that there are much easier ways to do things, especially for systems they use only occasionally. This kind of proactive action helps the user to get help just when he or she needs it.

Level 4 IT departments use engagement metrics to track the users across their systems. It allows them to see who needs training, which business units are the least engaged and why, and which business units generate the most errors. These analyses help them devise ways to either train the users, improve the system, or simply advertise useful but little-known functionalities.

Building engagement metrics

Several systems help with tracking and measuring user engagement. Although helpful, these systems can quickly become expensive.

Level 4 IT departments don't necessarily use complex subsystems. They often make do with what they have, and most systems already come with various user-engagement metrics:

- Login activity
- Record ownership
- Security profiles
- User activity reports

These metrics can be used as good starting points to develop engagement metrics. For example, login activity tells us what kind of user they are (daily use, weekly must-do, occasional query, etc.). Comparing a user's login activity to their peers can help define if they are using a system more or less.

Record ownership can also help. Building an activity report shows just how active the user is in the system. For example, in a document-management system, a report might show the number of documents created by month, the number of documents consulted, etc. It gives a rough approximation of the level and type of usage.

Am I using it well?

Business managers don't have the time to evaluate whether each of their employees is a proficient user. They find it difficult enough trying to keep up with all the operational components of their role. But that doesn't mean they are not interested.

Everyone is trying to do more with less, and system productivity is an important factor. Managers that get engagement data can better manage their employees' performance.

Level 4 IT departments sit down with managers and discuss the levels of user engagement. An engineering organization barely using the document-management system might find that it is simply a matter of training the users or that the system doesn't address user needs, something that can be fixed.

Analyzing usage patterns and variances across business units can help everyone become better, more engaged users.

Becoming Level 4: User engagement

How much do you know about your users? If you are like most IT departments, you know very little about them.

When we do user-satisfaction surveys with our clients, we always ask for the same information: a list of users with as much information as the client has on them. This includes business unit, date of hire, date of birth, number of help-desk requests, physical location, type of equipment, etc. In more than 50 percent of cases, we get stuck on the first one: business unit. IT cannot get us a list of its users by business unit without having to reach out to HR. It would seem like the most basic thing to know about users, but the reality is that IT has never had to know a whole lot about them. That is, until now.

We will build a plan to better understand your users. We will use that understanding to adapt IT services, improve satisfaction, and promote engagement.

Why engagement?
In a nutshell, user engagement is the amount of time and effort users put toward using their systems above and beyond the minimum necessary to do their job. A user with a low level of engagement will do

the minimum of tasks required in the system. This typically will be limited to transaction, process-type activities: enter a sales order, fill out a timesheet, etc.

The problem is that the systems that tend to make a big difference to the organization are not transactional systems. They are collaboration- and analytical-type systems. The use of these systems is not mandatory. Nothing will happen if a sales person fails to log every single calls he makes in the company's customer relationship management (CRM). Nothing will break if a finance-team member doesn't put his new analysis model into the document-management system. But there will also be no benefits. No one will look at the CRM because they know the information is incomplete. Someone else will build a model identical to the one just developed by finance, simply because he or she didn't know it exists.

This is where the real value of these systems comes from, but they require engaged users to work. Level 4 IT departments understand they have a critical role to play in engaging users.

Measuring engagement
Measuring engagement is always a challenge. After all, what is engagement? Is someone logging into the ERP system to fill out his or her weekly timesheet an engaged user? Is someone working at inputting payables all day engaged?

We like to use the term *acts of engagement* to define the different types of engagement.

Acts of engagement
An act of engagement is an activity a user could perform in a system that can be measured. Here are a few examples of acts of engagement for a CRM system:

- Logging in to the system

- Adding a customer

- Adding an order

- Logging a customer service call

- Adding a lead

- Entering a new interaction with a lead

- Consulting a sales report

- Consulting a client's history

- Analyzing win rate by lead type

- Consulting a list of cold leads to reactivate them

Today, CRM systems can easily track all of these actions, but these actions are not all equal. Some have more value or represent a more "engaged" user than others. After all, I don't have a choice about whether to add a new customer to the system or else they won't be able to put orders through. We call these activities *ritual compliance*. The user will do the minimum required to get by.

We call the next category of actions *strategic compliance*. These actions have no inherent value to the user but are associated with something that does have value. For example, a salesperson might enter new leads into the system simply to look good in the weekly activity report.

Finally, there are some actions that users find intrinsically valuable in their day-to-day work. They may help users close deals or build better relationships with their clients, for example. We call them *engagement actions*.

Let's take a look at our acts of engagement in these categories:

Category	Acts of engagement
Ritual compliance	• Logging in to the system • Adding a customer • Adding an order • Logging a customer service call
Strategic compliance	• Adding a lead • Entering a new interaction with a lead • Consulting a sales report
Engagement	• Consulting a client's history • Analyzing win rate by lead type • Consulting list of cold leads to reactivate them

We see that not all actions have the same value. Employees who enter sales orders all day will be in the ritual compliance zone. They do the action simply because their work requires them to do it, not because they find inherent value in it.

The problem with acts of engagement is that they vary significantly from one system to another. They even vary from one type of user to another. We cannot expect all users to use the system in the same way.

Roles

This is why we use the concept of roles to define just how a user would use the system in an ideal world. Let's continue on our CRM example.

Three types of roles typically use a CRM: a salesperson who manages leads and clients, a sales manager who tracks salespeople's performance, and a customer service agent who tracks interactions. Each of these roles has a distinct usage pattern.

Salesperson	Sales Manager	Customer Service
Enters new leads (daily)	Consults reports (daily)	Consults client activity (daily)
Adds activities for leads (daily)	Assigns quotas and sales targets (monthly)	Enters new orders (daily)
Consults reports (weekly)		Enters service requests (daily)

We see that the salesperson is much more preoccupied with entering and managing leads and will periodically consult reports tracking his or her performance (and bonuses). On the other hand, the sales manager doesn't enter any new information but is an avid report reader. Finally, the customer service agent consults and updates client files daily. These represent our ideal usage patterns, each with ritual compliance, strategic compliance, and engagement actions.

We now have a starting point to measure individual users. When we compare the engagement actions of two salespersons, we can see below that Salesperson 1 uses the system as planned, but Salesperson 2 performs only mandatory tasks. He or she doesn't use the system reports. This person uses the system out of necessity and is less likely to be engaged with the system than Salesperson 1. The day a sales manager becomes less diligent about tracking compliance, the use of the system will go out the window.

Actions	Profile	Salesperson 1	Salesperson 2
New leads per day	2	2	1
Activities per day	10	12	2
Reports consulted per week	2	3	0
Engagement		High	Low

Engagement patterns

Acts of engagement are one thing, but *when* people engage with an application can also tell us a lot about it. Let's consider the example of two different salespersons. We've looked at the number of times they accessed their CRM system for a given week. They both had twenty-six acts of engagement (consult a file, add a client, etc.).

But Salesperson 1 consults the system almost every day while Salesperson 2 does all of his work on Friday. If we were to ask the users, chances are Salesperson 1 would find more value in the system, using it continually as part of her day-to-day activities. Salesperson 2 probably considers the CRM as merely "paperwork" to make his boss happy. The rest of the time, he takes notes in his agenda or on paper scraps, napkins, etc. Or he uses a different system that is much better suited to his needs and transfers the information on Fridays.

The same number of engagement acts doesn't lead to the same level of engagement. The key, of course, is to understand what the engagement pattern should look like for any given individual. It might make sense to use some applications only on Fridays.

System-by-system approach

Measuring engagement is thus something that is specific to each system. It requires defining ideal profiles and measuring against them. This represents a lot of work, and while it is valuable for the bigger systems, it quickly becomes difficult to accomplish for each and every smaller system out there.

An alternative is simply to measure the number of times people use the system. This metric is typically very easy to find (login records or activity records) and provides a rough idea of whether people are using the system, and when.

We often see systems with one hundred registered users being used by fewer than twenty users in any given month. Either the other eighty shouldn't have access to the system in the first place (cost of licenses), or they failed to find the value they were looking for.

Measuring engagement might seem like a lot of work, but it's the only way to ensure that your systems are actually providing value to the organization.

Understanding your users

Once the Basics are being measured, we can start better understanding the users themselves. We often get asked: "Shouldn't you understand the users before you start doing anything?" And of course, it seems as if that would make a lot of sense. But the reality is that few IT departments know enough about their users to make use of the information. It would take weeks or months of interviews, research, and focus groups to gain a viable understanding. User-satisfaction surveys can get you that understanding in merely a few days.

If I ask you to think about your users, chances are, you have a very specific user-type who comes to mind. Perhaps you're thinking of the administrative assistant who continually calls for help about the Office productivity suite, or the engineer who keeps changing the setup. We have a very biased view of users, caused by our own relationship with IT and by our day-to-day interactions. Making decisions about users based on this flawed perception is not only counterproductive, but dangerous.

The reality is that your users vary greatly from one another. They have different objectives in their use of technology, in how they work, and in how much change they can take. Treating everyone the same way simply doesn't work. This is something that Level 4 IT departments understand.

To better know users, it is useful to create personas, or imaginary users, based on various criteria.

Example of persona:

Sylvie Admin	
Name	Sylvie Admin
Age	Middle-aged
IT and Internet	Low
Use of software	Medium
Using mobile - tablet apps	Low
Social networks	Low
User experience goals	Simplicity
Device and platform	Desktop, image #des7801
Anxiety tolerance	Low
Description	Sylvie Admin performs repetitive tasks, entering sales orders or interacting with customers. She is very proficient in a small subset of functionalities in select applications. She becomes quickly overwhelmed when trying to do something new.
Training	Prefers formal training

John Engineer	
Name	John Engineer
Age	Mid-adulthood
IT and Internet	High
Use of software	Medium
Using mobile - tablet apps	High
Social networks	Medium
User experience goals	Control
Device and platform	Desktop, image #des8132
Anxiety tolerance	Medium
Description	John Engineer spends a considerable amount of time tweaking his work environment, changing settings, and installing applications to make his work more productive. Comfortable with complex environments, he tends to support himself.
Training	Prefers to use documentation and own resources (Internet)

Building personas

It is easy to get lost in the details when building user personas. After all, you could use all sorts of information you have available to the point where you could have dozens of different combinations. The key is not to focus on what information you have, but on what makes users different.

Starting from the user-satisfaction survey

A good starting point is the user satisfaction survey you've been running. It provides a wealth of information about how happy users are with their IT services. You can use that information to start making sense of what drives satisfaction.

Let's take an easy example and say the engineering department's satisfaction level is much lower than finance's. We can assume that engineering has much different needs from finance, which makes sense. But another explanation could be that engineering contains a different type of user altogether. While finance tends to hire technology-averse technicians to do routine work, engineering hires technology-savvy, highly educated users for knowledge work. Their expectations toward their equipment will differ drastically. While one will want equipment that is easy to use, the other will want control of the machines.

Education is not the only factor. Age is important as well. Twenty-somethings tend to feel a lot more comfortable with mobile devices and social networks than fifty-somethings. The way younger people learn and work is also dramatically different; they are often more efficient in a high-interrupt environment and with sharing information.

Analyzing your user satisfaction using different variables allows us to see which user patterns emerge and gives us a nice starting point.

Choosing equipment

Personas are useful when selecting computers because each persona will tend to have slightly different needs and require a different equipment type. A high-travel persona will probably require a small, lightweight laptop or tablet that is easily carried while a finance Excel jockey will require a somewhat powerful machine with multiple screens to view entire spreadsheets at once.

Choosing software

Both as a consultant for Gartner and as a CIO, I've participated in countless product evaluations for new software. And I'm ashamed to say that very few times did I take into account the personas of those who would be using it. I've looked at architecture, technology, databases, functionalities, and vendor viability. But never did I consider that someone would employ it to do a job day in and day out.

Take the choice of ERP, for example. Some vendors are well-known to be very complete solutions but complex to use. While they allow a lot of functionality, their adoption tends to remain low because users feel uncomfortable with them. We should choose the solution as if we were the users. Millions of dollars are wasted in picking the right solution for the wrong people.

Don't go overboard

Personas represent a general picture of the user segment, not an actual person. It is tempting to develop personas to the point where their background story is very real. This stops becoming useful very quickly. Instead, the persona development process should be very quick. What are the top characteristics that distinguish this user from others? Knowing they tend to own a dog doesn't add a lot of value, but understanding that they use social media heavily will help choose or develop new applications.

Personas are an approximation. When trying to assign users to personas, some will fit well in multiple categories. Pick one. Don't feel the need to agonize over or develop so many personas that they stop being useful.

How many personas?

The rule of thumb is seven. If you choose more, it becomes difficult to remember them by heart. But choose less, and they become too generic.

Get the template

Get the template for user personas at:

GreenElephantTeam.com/BVIT

Recognition

An easy way to motivate users and engage them is to recognize their contributions.

Participating in knowledge-sharing and collaboration systems requires quite a bit of time and personal investment. And the obvious question is, "What's in it for me? Everyone else will make use of my knowledge and support, and I will never get the credit."

Social platforms like Facebook and Reddit provide recognition through the formation of a number of friends or by giving scores based on contributions. It becomes very obvious who is highly engaged in the platform and who isn't.

Systematizing recognition helps reassure users that the time and energy they spend sharing their expertise will be obvious to the people that matter: their bosses.

Training users

This is the part of the plan in which I receive the most resistance from my clients. Everyone agrees with the need to provide a solid infrastructure. That's a given. Some are reluctant to measure satisfaction, but most end up seeing the need. But training? Isn't this HR's or the business's responsibility? It isn't enough that we provide the applications—now we have to hold the users' hands as well?

As we've seen, Level 4 IT departments all say, "Yes, it is our responsibility." And the reason is simple: if users lack the skills to use the applications, they will not derive any value from them. Simply making the systems available is no longer enough.

Types of training

Let's look at the different types of training:

Traditional training:

- **Live training (classroom or web):** Costly and inefficient. Useful to present a new major change (like an ERP, for example) and the availability of concepts. Retention tends to be poor due to information overload.

- **Self-paced training:** Web-based approaches reduce the cost of training. Several courses are already available. Few users have the discipline to take training on themselves.

- **Super-user lead training:** Developing a network of super-users to train other employees. Although useful, super-users are often too busy to perform this role adequately.

Less traditional training:

- **Lunch-and-learn:** Quick sessions during lunchtime to cover a topic of interest to users. The unstructured, short, and casual approach makes it appealing to users. Free pizza always helps.

- **Video capsules:** Short capsules on how to perform specific tasks. Helps answer immediate questions for users.

- **In-application training:** More and more popular with commercial providers. Includes training directly in the application through users' onboarding process and reminders. Very high relevance, as users are trained while using the tool.

IT departments have focused mostly on traditional training methods which are typically used when new systems are deployed. The problem is that retraining current employees or training new employees is difficult to do live, and the development of training courses is expensive and time-consuming.

While these training activities have their place, Level 4 IT departments use less-traditional approaches focused on ongoing developmental training very successfully. For example, a monthly lunch-and-learn session on office products helps everyone interested consider their proficiency and learn about new functionalities to improve productivity. In-application training can show users new reports that they might not have known existed.

The overall theme here is that training doesn't have to be an elaborate, painful process. Training should be continual, light, and adapted to the users' evolving needs.

Defining training needs

How does one find out what kind of training users need? There are two ways, really. The first is to look at the requests your help-desk is receiving. Chances are, users call in with requests for help on a lot of training-related issues. A simple conversation with your help-desk staff will probably uncover dozens of training needs. Analyzing the help-desk's tickets provides a wealth of information about users' training needs, as well.

Helping users help each other

My daughter is a big fan of Minecraft, a computer-based survival game in which you gather and transform natural resources to build advanced tools and infrastructure. Starting with only your bare hands, you chop down trees to craft pickaxes, which in turn allows you to mine for metals, etc.

It can quickly become very complicated. Furthermore, the user community has developed a series of add-ons (or "mods") to further enhance the game. But installing these mods and using them can be very difficult for a dad like me.

Fortunately, Minecraft helps their users—not through great support (though it is pretty good), but through a very active user community. Players regularly participate in discussion forums, post how-to videos on YouTube, and answer each other's questions, all in the name of furthering the game. The most active contributors get ranks recognizing their contributions next to their names. When a high-ranking player posts a response, you know you can trust him or her. This is the perfect definition of an engaged user.

After looking for a solution to a particularly difficult problem, my daughter decided that the how-to videos she'd viewed weren't clear enough. She took it upon herself to record her own video, post it on YouTube, and share it with others on the forums. And she's only ten years old.

Often, the biggest contribution IT can make to users is to put them in touch with each other and get out of the way. Engaged users are happy to learn more about their systems, to share their experiences, and to support one another. But, to do so, they need a platform—a way to contact each other and share.

We often limit what is available to the users. We want to make sure we control the message; that the training is appropriate and "corporate." But often, what users want is a quick-and-dirty screenshot or video from someone else who had the same problem and resolved it.

Engagement

What about the needs users might not realize they have? Systems are complex, and training is often done all at once, leading users to forget a great deal of what they've been taught. It's easy for them to simply be unaware that something is possible.

ERPs are a great example of this. ERP systems tend to be complex and require considerable training. It can take weeks for users to learn how to perform just the basic day-to-day tasks required of them. But what about the wealth of other functionalities and reports that are available, but that they simply aren't aware of? Perhaps their initial training covered these subjects, but they have long since forgotten about them. By analyzing the usage patterns of the users, an IT leader can spot the functionalities that aren't being used and the reports that aren't being generated and then investigate. Comparing different users also helps. If two accounts-payable clerks show very different usage patterns, it's worthwhile to investigate whether retraining one of them makes sense.

3. Play your role

Understanding the role

Jean had just been hired as the new CIO of a large, family-owned business. He had built a successful career as an IT manager for various public organizations and felt he would have greater impact working for a private company. The smaller size would allow him to move quickly and influence the company's direction with the owner.

But things got off on the wrong foot when Jean started scheduling meetings with the business executives. One after the other, they would cancel at the last minute. None of them were responsive to e-mails or phone calls, either.

When he finally got a face-to-face, he was surprised by the executive's attitude: "I don't get why you're asking all these questions. Business strategy isn't your responsibility—just get our systems working."

Jean was under the impression that business strategy was exactly his responsibility—at least, in whatever way he could contribute to it.

But these executives were uninterested in having these discussions with him.

Jean had clearly misunderstood the expectations for his role. He had thought he would be playing the role of a partner, or at least have some business input. But he had been relegated back to the role of an order-taker.

Of course, Jean didn't stay long at this company. He quickly left for an organization where he could enjoy more influence.

Value and alignment
We'd like to think that high-value IT departments all play a strategic role within their organizations—that they sit at the executive table and drive strategies and orientations.

Although that's the case for several, it is not a prerequisite for delivering business value. In fact, the most important part is not the role IT plays, but whether the role is in line with the business's expectations.

We'll examine the four different roles IT can play in an organization and the importance of alignment.

> **How Level 4 IT departments play their role**
>
> Level 4 IT departments play their role in four ways:
>
> 1. They understand their current and expected personality profiles.
> 2. They align their team.
> 3. They align the vision.
> 4. They align the business.

1. Personality profiles

IT departments can be categorized into four distinct personality profiles. These profiles have an impact on the perception of IT within the organization and also on the behavior of the IT team on a day-to-day basis.

We use two different dimensions to define personality profiles:

Service orientation: Service orientation represents the organization's focus on customer service. Some organizations manage IT as a cost center and want to minimize interactions with the users, while others try to be ultra-responsive to the users' needs.

Business orientation: Business orientation measures the IT team's level of business understanding. Some IT departments simply deliver generic IT services, while others possess a deep understanding of the business issues and propose technology solutions to address them.

The combination of service orientation (vertical axis) and business orientation (horizontal axis) gives us four distinct personality profiles.

Business Orientation

The Accountant

Accountants believe IT is a necessary evil, something that is essential but must be tightly managed. They also worry that users might abuse or steal IT resources if left on their own. They believe that controlling users is essential to controlling costs.

Accountants thrive in centralized environments, for example, manufacturing companies, where users tend to have little knowledge or need for IT in their day-to-day work.

Walmart shows us the best example of the Accountant personality. Walmart's goal is to reduce prices (and costs). It does not provide a nice shopping ambiance or advice, but focuses on providing everyday low prices—and it is proud of this focus.

The Butler

Butlers strongly desire to serve their users. They realize that their organization depends on them and are more than willing to be strong support players. They treat every user like a paying customer, believing that users should be able to rely on IT and receive satisfaction from the services provided.

Butlers thrive in areas in which users are very technology-knowledgeable and demanding, such as engineering, pharmaceuticals, or design.

Starbucks comes to mind when we think of the Butler. Starbucks provides great service, but at a price. It adapts its ambiance throughout the day so you can get your caffeine fix quickly in the morning, catch up on work during the day, or finish off a date in the evening. But Starbucks will not stop you after eight coffees. It responds to requests; it doesn't help you achieve your objectives.

The Nanny

Nannies are the driving force behind the adoption of technologies within their organizations. Their unique understanding of business and technology lends them a keen strategic view.

Just like a real nanny, they will guide the users in the right direction, ensuring they are productive while obeying the rules.

The Nanny's relentless focus on improving business processes often results in higher IT costs, but those are always justified with a great return on investments.

Nannies thrive in environments where the users have limited to little knowledge of technology. The retail sector is a great example, where the turnover rate at the store level can be as high as 40 percent per year.

The best example of a Nanny is Apple. Apple doesn't consult anyone before coming up with new products. It doesn't apologize when it removes features or drops product lines. It believes it knows what we want better than we do. And, often, it is right.

The Agent

Agents believe that IT can drive their organization to become more competitive. They believe they need to be involved in the majority of business initiatives to have a beneficial impact.

We find Agents in organizations that have recognized the strategic role that IT can play. Financial services and insurance companies are great examples of places we can find Agents.

When we think of Agents, we think of Weight Watchers. Weight Watchers' mission is to help people reach and maintain a healthy weight. It does so by simplifying calorie counting (using points) and providing support groups and tools. It focuses not on the means, but on the results. And that is the main difference with Agents—they focus on helping their clients reach their objectives through whatever means it takes.

Which one is best?

When we look at this type of chart, it is easy to believe that the upper-right category is the best (the Agent). In fact, when I pose the question to IT leaders, 58 percent say they are a Nanny. But, when I talk to the business executives, only 14 percent agree with them.

The reality is a little different. The best position is not the upper-right quadrant. The best position is the one the business expects.

An organization that focuses on cost control will expect an Accountant. The manufacturing sector is a great example. They expect IT to be cheap and don't believe that technology can play a major role (although this is changing).

A CIO who comes in and tries to behave as an Agent or a Nanny (like our example earlier) will get turned down pretty quickly.

But a retail organization that sees a 40 percent employee turnover rate will expect a Nanny. It will want someone capable of imposing processes and standards through systems. It will deem someone behaving as a Butler and delivering on every request as too "weak" and providing too little leadership.

Level 4 IT departments recognize the expected role and adapt themselves to fulfill it.

We call this concept *alignment*, but we'll see that there are actually three types of alignment.

Alignment

When we hear about alignment, we typically look at it from a budget perspective: Are the IT projects in line with the priorities of the organization?

Of course, this concept of alignment is important, but oddly enough, it is not the most important. In fact, we see that three types of alignment influence IT's business value:

- Team alignment
- Vision alignment
- Business alignment

2. Team alignment

Does everyone in your team understand and agree with their role?

When we ask IT team members what role IT plays in their organization, we often receive a variety of answers. Some think that IT should play a commanding role (a Nanny), while others believe IT should answer requests (a Butler).

When team members don't agree on their role, it becomes difficult to present a unified front to the users and to the business, resulting in users calling certain individuals in IT directly. They don't trust anyone else to behave as they think IT should.

Level 4 IT departments display high levels of agreement on their role. Most of their IT members not only agree but also understand what their role means on a day-to-day basis.

3. Vision alignment

The team is aligned, but does it match the IT leader's vision?

We often see a mismatch between what the team believes its role should be and what the IT leader wants.

IT leaders tend to want to provide a high level of service and play a strategic role in the organization. However, team members tend to be busy and overworked, and only want to focus on the essentials. They believe they lack the capacity to do more "relationship" or "strategic" work.

This causes frustration both within the team and with the IT leader. Each feels the other doesn't understand the realities of the organization.

It also creates frustration within the business. The IT leader makes commitments that his or her team cannot deliver or reminds everyone of the importance of service while the help-desk has a hard time dealing with the call volume.

Level 4 IT departments possess a strong vision alignment. The IT leaders spend plenty of time communicating their vision over and over again. They try to clarify what specific behaviors are expected on a day-to-day basis for each role. Saying "Provide great customer service!" isn't enough. It needs to be reinforced with specific coaching, examples, and recognition.

What happens when IT cares more than the business?

Mike was leading a difficult IT organization. An alternative energy operator, the company specialized in turning troubled energy development projects into success stories.

But the organization was spread out between two very different countries, each with their own ways of doing things. Mike did his best to standardize technology between the two groups, but, one day, things became difficult.

"The North American group wants to change the control center for their energy production facilities," Mike said, "but it is such a big investment that it would make sense to involve the European division on this to save costs."

The problem was that no one else in the organization shared Mike's mission to standardize. The president and executive understood the benefits of standardization, but they also wanted to move quickly and avoid getting bogged down.

Mike was the only one who cared about standardization. The problem was that he cared so much, he slowed down initiatives. He tried to make every project a corporate project, up to the point where the different divisions started doing their own things. They were trying to reduce the need for IT by purchasing managed technology solutions, cutting IT out of the picture.

By trying to enforce a corporate standard, Mike drove the divisions away.

They perceived Mike as a show-stopper, an obstacle to progress. The divisions were trying to compete in a difficult environment, and their partner was not helping at all.

Mike did all this in the name of "corporate objectives," which the corporation did not share.

4. Business alignment

The team and the vision are aligned, great. But does the alignment match the expectations of the business?

IT often gives itself "missions" based on what it feels it must do. This mission might be to reduce costs wherever possible, or it might be to standardize everything on one platform.

Problems arise when the mission doesn't match what the organization wants. The business might not be concerned about centralizing everything (like in our previous example); perhaps all it wants are smooth operations.

This alignment is not only felt in the budget or projects, but is also seen in the behavior of the IT team. IT teams that won't talk about a project until a project request has been logged cannot pretend to be a Butler or an Agent. A team that doesn't spend time understanding the business cannot pretend to be a Nanny or an Agent.

We must also consider the fact that the "business" doesn't exist. We have a series of business units and key stakeholders that may all have different expectations for the role of IT. Finance might expect IT to act as a Nanny to help enforce corporate policies. Meanwhile, sales wants a Butler to install new systems and tools.

Level 4 IT departments treat each business unit as an individual entity with its own priorities and objectives. They make a sustained effort to understand their operations and constraints, and they adapt their role based on what each business unit expects.

Changing expectations
What if you don't agree with the role expected of IT?

IT leaders face one of the biggest challenges when attempting to contribute to the business. If the business doesn't let IT sit at the executive table, many reasons may exist:

- The business leaders don't understand the possible contribution IT can make.
- The business leaders don't believe IT can execute.
- The business leaders don't believe IT understands the business.
- The business leaders had bad experiences in the past.

It is easy to get pigeonholed by a false perception of IT's capabilities. In fact, many IT leaders never get past this point.

Level 4 IT departments don't let the initial expectations define their roles. They understand that perception is often reality but also that perceptions can be changed.

They make a conscious effort to assess the position of each major business unit and stakeholder. They devise a plan to change the perception of IT and the expectations for its role.

A seat at the executive table is earned, not given.

Becoming Level 4: Playing your role

An important part of playing your role consists of setting the right expectations in the first place. We've already covered that satisfaction equals the difference between the service delivered and the service expected. No matter how well we serve the organization, it will never be satisfied if its expectations are unrealistic.

We will see how we can set the correct expectations with the users, the business leaders, and finally the IT team.

Setting expectations with the users

We've seen how users form expectations through different mechanisms: their prior employment, their own experience as consumers, and the last few interactions with your service. This can be a dangerous combination leading to wild differences between users. Someone who worked for a very mature company might come to expect a lot from the support and equipment received, while someone from a technology-averse company will be delighted to get a working computer.

Left unmanaged, it would be impossible for IT to consistently meet these expectations. Some users would be very satisfied, some would be very dissatisfied, and there would be no way to explain why. This is why it is critical to manage users' expectations before they start using your service.

The best moment to set expectations is right when users are hired. As you onboard them and provide them with their equipment and access, it is wise to inform them of the different IT service levels. This includes support and help-desk response time, for example, but also things like how long they will have their computer, how they can get (or cannot get) other software and devices, what they can and cannot install, etc.

The next best time is when they ask for service. A reminder at every interaction helps reset expectations, proving especially useful as time goes by and users experience higher levels of service. Someone who is used to getting his or her call answered in only a few rings will be dissatisfied when it takes longer. But reminding the user of what should be expected while on hold helps to reset expectations right away.

It may be tempting to set very low expectations in order to consistently over-deliver. This way, we look like a hero every time. But, in fact, this works only once. Afterward, people will reset their expectations to your real service levels and disregard any attempt you make to steer their expectations to a different level. Additionally, if expectations are too low, users will fail to realize the added value they receive above and beyond the expected levels. People find it difficult to recognize value that is too far above their expectations.

Setting expectations with the business units

Just as we need to set user expectations regarding the basic services we provide, we must also set expectations for the business unit or business services. These services are typically related to the development and evolution of new systems and processes.

Service catalogs

Service catalogs are often used to help set the business's expectations. In theory, a service catalog should list all of the services IT provides, along with the associated service levels. Business leaders would know exactly what, when, and how they would receive their services and would be able to compare them against the service levels. If anyone wanted something that was not in the catalog, they would need to negotiate separately.

Although it sounds great in theory, most service catalogs miss the mark.

I'm the one responsible for auto maintenance in my household. No, that doesn't mean I actually know anything about mechanics; it just means that I'm the one who gets the car to the dealership. My wife hates going to the dealership. She believes they are always trying to oversell her on unnecessary services—and, because she knows nothing about cars, she has no choice but to accept. Her thinking is that, because I'm a man and know a little bit more about cars than she does, I won't face the same challenges. But she's wrong.

Last year I went to the dealership with my older car and asked for maintenance. The mechanic in charge started asking me all sorts of questions: "Do you want synthetic oil? Are we changing the air filter?" And they are very transparent. Each and every one of their services is listed and priced. I know exactly what I'm buying. The problem is, I don't know if I need it, so I'm stuck making a decision on something I know little about.

My wife has since bought a new car, and I'm still responsible for maintenance. But, this time, maintenance was included in the car's purchase price. All of the cars they sell come with four free years of maintenance. So, when I showed up at the garage, they had only one question for me: "Will you be waiting here, or do you need a courtesy car?" They are the experts on that particular car; they know what they have to do. They don't need me to make decisions on something that is clearly not my specialty.

And that is the problem with most service catalogs. They list services that few people really understand. They ask the business leaders to make choices without understanding the consequences. I've seen service catalogs that listed different development times depending on the programming language they used. How is a business leader supposed to decide?

Service catalogs are best used for high-volume, standardized services, such as help-desk and equipment. Projects and development obtain little value from being listed in service catalogs and might even confuse more than help.

Industry knowledge

How much do you know about the business? And what about the industry? When I talk to IT leaders, they often mention that they would like to be an Agent in the IT personality profile (high service orientation and high business orientation). But playing on the right-hand side of the quadrants comes with different expectations for just how much the organization understands both the business it serves and the industry it is a part of.

How much do you really know about your business? Can you explain its mission, its major processes, and its constraints? Would you be able to lead a different business unit if you were promoted? Too often, IT leaders focus on getting expertise in their own field and fail to really understand their organization. But an organization expecting an Agent (high service orientation, high business orientation) or a Nanny (low service orientation, high business orientation) dramatically changes IT's level of understanding and involvement in the business. Can you make educated guesses of the likely impact of an increase in the value of your currency? Or an interest-rate increase?

The same applies to industry knowledge. Do you understand the trends that affect your industry (whether related to IT or not)? What are the likely moves of your competitors (or peers)? Who is most likely to acquire whom? What are the next products/services that are likely to have an impact? What regulations can possibly help/become an obstacle? Understanding the industry also means knowing who the key players are and tracking their progress.

It's one thing for the IT leader to understand these concepts, but do the other IT department personnel understand them as well? Do they spend time tracking the industry and its peers?

If you're not ready to do this, both as a department and as an individual, then it is important to set the right expectations with the business. Let's not pretend that you want to be a Nanny or an Agent if you're not interested in or capable of developing your business orientation.

Setting expectations with the team

One of the ways people form expectations is through visual cues—in our case, how people look. I once worked with an organization that considered itself to be very creative. Business people wore leather pants and sported red mohawks. They not only tolerated but also encouraged people to express their creativity through their dress. The IT team took the cue to do the same and dressed very casually. I was surprised to see everyone, including the vice-president (VP), wearing jeans and old t-shirts. Not the cool old vintage t-shirts, but the really old, don't-even-use-them-as-pajamas type. In every respect, they dressed similar to the business—except that they didn't look creative; they looked like slobs.

The business team may have been wearing jeans and leather jackets, but their looks resulted from an elaborate thinking process. Everyone put considerable effort into making their appearance a reflection of their personality. The business creative with a twelve-inch mohawk spent a lot of time every morning fixing himself up. On the other hand, the IT team looked like they grabbed whatever was on the floor and put it on to go to work. They thought they were blending in, but, in fact, their appearance was a serious disconnect.

People use visual cues to set expectations. If someone arrives to fix your computer looking like this, chances are, you won't expect much from his performance. You might even double-check everything afterward to ensure he didn't create problems. Even if he did an amazing job, you wouldn't recognize it, as people have a hard time readjusting their expectations even in the light of the actual performance. You cannot satisfy someone who has very low expectations.

Did you set the expectations for your team as to what is considered appropriate business attire? Probably not. After all, they are all professionals; they should know how to dress themselves. You shouldn't have to go into this level of detail. Turns out, you do.

IT employees are the living and breathing representations of the IT brand. And, as we've seen, the value of IT is its brand. Do your employees contribute to your brand, or are they tarnishing it? I'm using the example of uniforms, but it applies to many elements of the interaction process: the way people answer calls, their voicemail, etc.

If you don't spend time setting expectations with your team, you might be surprised at the wide range of variations you will find. I've known people who were constantly late for meetings, to the point where it became a joke. It also cost one person a promotion, as his boss was thinking, "If he can't manage his schedule, how can he manage a department?"

Setting expectations is one thing, but maintaining them is another. It requires calling out every single instance of noncompliance you find, which can quickly become taxing. I had a habit of closing the door when a meeting started so that no one else could come in. Sometimes, I wanted to open the door badly because I needed a particular person at the meeting. However, I forced myself to keep them out, and soon no one showed up late anymore. I also regularly walked by the technical support labs to check for cleanliness. Were there boxes and wires everywhere, or was everything tidy? By enforcing a constantly clean environment with frequent visits, I was able to drive home the importance of appearances.

4. Create partnerships

Being a partner is more than just a title

When I worked as a CIO, one of the HR representatives came to introduce himself. He happily told me that he was my "business partner," and I was surprised to see this actual title on his business card.

He went on to say that he would like to sit in on all my departmental meetings and remain aware of all my objectives and strategies.

Perhaps it was a bad day for me, but I felt like being a little difficult, so I asked him to explain further what being a partner meant to him. He droned on and on about how he would be my right-hand man for all things HR-related.

I asked him first if he could resolve an issue with my retirement contribution plan. It seemed that my membership form had been buried under someone's desk for six months and was going nowhere.

My "partner" flatly replied that this was not something he would handle and that I needed to contact someone else in HR to resolve this. His role was strategic, not operational.

I thanked him profusely and proceeded to never call him again.

Being a partner is a lot of work

I find it an interesting exercise to look at the resumes of IT leaders on LinkedIn. I always see some form of "be a partner to the business" or "act as a strategic partner." I always want to reach for the phone and call a few business leaders to ask them if so-and-so is really a partner to them.

It seems that the definition of "being a partner" is something very flexible. It swings from being light acquaintances to being practically married.

But you cannot assign yourself as a partner. Being a partner is something that is earned, that is given by the other person. A partnership is something we build over time.

How Level 4 IT departments create partnerships

Level 4 IT departments create partnerships in three ways:

1. They build and maintain trust.
2. They actively manage their partnerships.

Defining partnerships

Business relationships move through four different stages:

- **Emerging**: There is no relationship per se. The relationship is only beginning, and we barely know each other at the business level.

- **Transactional**: The level of trust is low. Most of the interactions between IT and the business unit revolve around specific requests.
- **Value-added:** The level of trust climbs as the business unit realizes the value that IT brings to solving its problems.
- **Strategic partner:** The highest level of trust. IT is part of the client's team, providing advice and assistance.

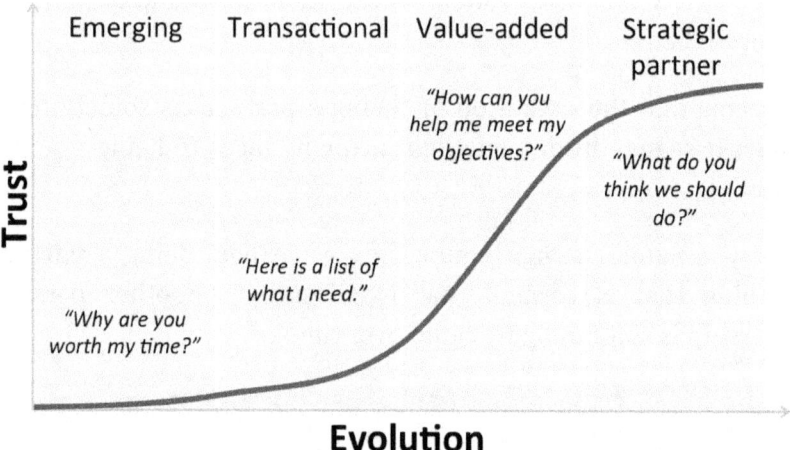

What distinguishes these different levels from each other is the amount of trust the partner places in the IT department.

We often think that, because we have a personal relationship, we have a business relationship. That's not the case at all. In fact, although a personal relationship can help, it by no means indicates a good business relationship. After all, we all know people we love to talk with but to whom we'd never give the keys to our house.

Level 4 IT departments work hard to build trust and navigate the partnership cycle. That doesn't mean they are a partner with all the business units of the organization, but it does mean they have plans to get there.

They regularly assess and track the relationship level with each business unit and stakeholder.

How trust is formed

Trust begins before your first contact with the person. It starts with your reputation and your department's reputation.

Organizations talk. A lot. Rumors spread like wildfires, and this is especially true when it comes to IT. People seem to particularly enjoy highlighting all the ways IT hasn't lived up to its role. Failed or late projects, defective equipment, calls that never get returned—these (true or not) all contribute to your reputation in the organization.

This is why Level 4 IT departments work hard to maintain their reputation. They take an active role in identifying rumors and issues before they spread. A user is dissatisfied? They will make sure to turn their horror story into a great turnaround story. Someone is spreading false rumors? The IT department will confront them to set the record straight. They actively defend their reputations.

But, of course, reputation is only the starting point. You then have to work to build the relationship.

1. Building trust

Two critical variables are involved in building trust:

1. Contact frequency

2. Making and meeting commitments

Contact frequency

Early relationships require a high level of contact frequency. We meet so many people in our business life that it is easy to forget someone. But contact frequency needs to be balanced with relevance. Calling someone to chat about the weather will do little to help the relationship.

As the relationship evolves, contact frequency tends to reduce, in favor of contact length. We spend more time in one-on-one meetings, lunches, or even off-site activities (golf, conferences, etc.). Because a base level of relationship exists, it is easier to distance contacts.

IT departments can go months at a time without direct contact with a specific group or business unit. We might contact them only when a problem happens. IT leaders often work on the premise of "no news is good news."

Level 4 IT departments disagree with this approach. They aim for a contact frequency of at least two per month. We do not include group meetings in these calculations (executive meetings, for example). We are talking about individual connections through meetings, phone calls, or e-mails.

These contacts reinforce the IT department's carefully constructed reputations. For example, they might give a heads-up on an upcoming initiative. They might give a quick status update on an ongoing issue. Or, they might touch base to make sure everything is progressing to their satisfaction. They never fail to get in touch.

Making and meeting commitments

Of course, having meetings with someone is not enough to build trust. You must also prove that you, and your organization, are reliable. One way to do that is to make small commitments—and, of course, keep them. "I'll get back to you on Monday about this." "Let me find out what John thinks of that." "Let me give you that information by Tuesday."

Commitments don't have to be large—no point in promising huge projects or benefits. A commitment can be the promise of information, a follow-up, or an investigation.

By making and keeping small commitments, you establish a pattern of reliability. You do what you say. This, in turn, increases your reputation and thus your level of trustworthiness.

Level 4 IT departments take a systematic approach to making and meeting commitments. They record every commitment they make (meeting notes, to dos, etc.). They understand that they cannot afford to miss even one of these commitments, especially at the beginning of a relationship. But this doesn't prevent them from making those commitments. They go out of their way to create opportunities to showcase that they are a reliable partner.

Losing trust

Political analysts agree that Bill Clinton has been one of the best politicians in the last few **decades**. The economy grew 4 percent per year under his terms. Unemployment steadily decreased. He helped broker a peace treaty in the Middle East. Regardless of where you lean politically, he did more for the economy, peace, and international relations than most.

Yet, that's not what we remember Bill Clinton for. We remember him for Monica Lewinsky and the cigar. A president who cheats on his wife is not a big deal in itself. Kennedy was known to have a relationship with Marilyn Monroe. The real problem was that Clinton lied about it and tried to redefine the word "sex" to cover his lies. Instead of coming clean, he ruined his reputation and his legacy.

There are four ways to lose trust:

Capabilities: failing to deliver projects or initiatives, failing to resolve problems or issues, being unpredictable in your service delivery.

Credibility: breaking the confidence bond, lying or talking behind someone's back.

Connectedness: failing to listen, lacking empathy, or failing to involve others in the decision-making process.

Reliability: failing to do what you said, being disorganized, or failing to follow up

Level 4 IT departments recognize the difficulty in building trust. As such, they work hard not to lose it. They make sure they do not make commitments they cannot meet. They never act in ways that might be seen as disrespectful to their partners, even in their own internal meetings. It is easy to lose trust—a lot easier than to earn it.

Building trust with a difficult department

The operation group of a company acquired less than two years earlier was operating independently. Now, we were asking them not only to work with the rest of the company, but to follow corporate IT standards. They were quite unhappy.

My first meeting with the VP in charge was difficult at best. His first reaction was: "I don't understand why you wasted money flying all the way here. I don't understand what you want." He was polite but distant.

I asked him about his business objectives, and he evaded the question, refusing to share anything that might come back to haunt him. Then I asked him about his IT issues, and I got the laundry list:

- The printer on the second floor keeps jamming.
- His assistant's computer is slow.
- The VGA cable in the conference room is too short.
- Etc.

I had a list of over thirty items like this. I left quite disappointed. I had expected a strategic meeting, a discussion of real business issues, and instead I got a laundry list of technicalities. If I had known, I would have sent a technician instead.

But I didn't shy away from the challenge. I took notes of all these issues and followed up on each one of them. I made sure the cable was replaced, the printer was fixed, and the computer was upgraded. And, if something couldn't be changed, I informed the VP.

Three months later, I met with him for the second time and reported on the status of all the items on his list. If he was impressed, he didn't show it. Instead, he gave me another laundry list. It was pretty clear he was testing me.

But I also didn't budge and tackled all the items on the second list as well.

This showed him I took this process seriously. I was here to help him out and to make his life easier. I could be trusted as a partner. As our relationship grew, so did our trust level. He started confiding on more strategic issues, sharing his pains and problems. We worked together to develop solutions, and, over time, we became real partners.

But none of this would have happened if I hadn't fixed the printer first.

2. Actively managing partnerships

"Failing to plan is planning to fail."

Commercial account managers understand the need to manage relationships. After all, vendors are compensated based on their ability to build trust and move products and services. For them, managing a relationships is a necessity—it's second nature.

But, when we talk about managing relationships with IT managers, we receive a look of disgust. "What do you mean, managing a relationship? It's not something we manage!"

Of course it is.

Business relationships don't happen by accident. Level 4 IT departments take a systematic approach to managing relationships. They copy commercial account managers.

For some people, developing a partnership plan seems unnatural. After all, do we plan relationships? Well, in the business world, we do.

If you interact with any vendor of importance, chances are it keeps a detailed account plan on you. It has identified the key decision-makers, the influencers, and the obstacles. It knows your issues and challenges, your decision-making process, and your budget. What you might have thought was a personal, friendly relationship is a planned and systematic interaction.

Having a plan to manage your relationships is not evil. It doesn't diminish the integrity of these relationships, either. What it does is focus your resources.

The difference between personal and business relationships

When we talk with IT leaders about business relationships, we often hear the same comments: "I have a great relationship with the business. We often go out for lunch, and we talk often."

Great. But having a great personal relationship doesn't mean you have a great business relationship.

This also means that you can develop a great business relationship even if you don't have a personal relationship.

It's about planning ALL relationships
When I ask an IT leader to tell me if he or she enjoys a good relationship with the business, he or she always responds, "Yes." But, when I go through each business unit one by one, I find it is not so much the case. It's not that they have a bad relationship; it's that they don't have one at all.

Becoming Level 4: Partnerships

We already talked about the fact that "the business" doesn't exist. It actually comprises a collection of business units or regions. Trying to treat the entire business as one big entity is not only difficult but counterproductive.

Each business unit has its own priorities, issues, and constraints. Although everyone follows a shared corporate strategy, many variations can be found at the departmental level.

For example, an organization might focus on increasing sales, but finance, production, and transportation might have little to do with this. In fact, they might play no part at all in the sales strategy, but by no means will they stay idle during this time. They will have their own objectives, which will need IT support.

Managing partnerships at the departmental level allows the IT department to get a global view of priorities and constraints. It allows IT to put corporate objectives in context and properly assign resources. Most importantly, it prevents IT from being blindsided by new priorities or projects.

To help IT with this task, we've developed the partnership plan, a concise document that lists the important information on each business unit. In only a few pages, you get an overview of the critical information.

Building the partnership plan

The first time we have to build a partnership plan can be especially difficult. Not because the concepts are strange (although they might be), but because we realize we know next to nothing about our partners.

I built a partnership plan with a client for their finance department. Historically, IT and finance have always been very close. But, when we built the plan, the client realized he knew little about finance. What were its objectives? Sure, he knew about the ones with an IT component, but he didn't know about the others. He didn't realize that meeting bank covenants was an ongoing struggle for finance and took a big part of its attention.

This is why the first iteration of the partnership contains very little. And that's fine. It is a starting point.

There are three distinct steps for managing partnerships. The first involves understanding your partner's priorities and constraints. Then, we can set specific objectives with each partner that either focus on the partner itself (serving others) or remain internally focused (serving ourselves). Finally, partnerships are managed over the long term. We will explore more details on each step and look at the concept of the partnership management plan.

To help us understand, we will use a logistics department as an example.

Step 1. Understand

The first step of the partnership management plan is to understand your partners. But what does this mean, exactly? In a nutshell, it means we understand what they do on a day-to-day basis.

Understanding our partners means obtaining the following information:

- The partners themselves: The departments, business units, or other elements of your organization.

- The stakeholders: The people in the different business units.

- Priorities: The goals, objectives, and constraints of each partner.

- Projects: The projects requested, approved, and executed for each partner.

Let's take a look at each one of them.

What exactly is a partner?

To answer that question, we'll refer to your organizational chart. Some organizations use departments as the key organizational structures, while others use regions. Business units and functional groups are also popular, and some use a combination of several elements (matrix structure).

The definition of your partners should follow your organizational chart, to keep things simple. We want to use the same terminology that your organization uses. Most organizations still use traditional departments (such as finance, HR, operations, logistics, etc.), and we will use this model for our examples. But we can easily replace them with regions, matrix structures, or projects.

Stakeholders

Just as there is no such thing as the business, there is also no such thing as a department. We build relationships with people, not with corporate entities. It is thus important to identify who the people are in each partner.

Stakeholders are the people who are part of the partner's organization. The most obvious is the business unit head or whoever is in charge of the department, but it doesn't stop there. Unless it is a small business unit, chances are, you will also deal with other people. The business unit might be large enough to contain various subgroups that require their own stakeholders.

Roles

Stakeholders are not all the same. They possess varying levels of authority and influence within their respective business units.

The head person of the partner (for example, the VP of sales) is usually the decision-maker, the only person with the final say about what's happening in the department. The decision-maker's contribution and support are essential, as nothing will get done without them. But decision-makers are not necessarily involved in the day-to-day work, having relegated that to the influencer.

The influencer maintains a strong relationship with the decision-maker. The decision-maker relies on the influencer to handle small matters, freeing the decision-maker to focus on other things. In some cases, the influencer will also possess some level of understanding of IT, even if just the industry trends in the applications used.

Fostering a good relationship with the decision-maker is important. However, this person might not want to have a relationship with you. He or she might prefer to have the influencer develop the relationship and get involved only when necessary.

IT departments tend to refuse this arrangement, preferring to deal with the head directly.

But the decision-maker might have relegated most of the operational matters, not just IT. The second-in-command might be

106

handling most of the operational decisions. Failing to involve this person would be a critical mistake.

To keep things simple, we assign a level of priority to each stakeholder. Decision-makers and heads are typically given a "high" level of priority; people we deal with operationally are "normal," while others are "low." This helps prioritize where efforts will be put forward in developing relationships. Someone given a low level of priority will probably not be interested in spending a lot of time with you, anyway.

Relationship status

As we've seen earlier, relationships go through four predictable states: emergent, transaction, value-added, and partnership. Knowing where you stand with each stakeholder helps you understand the relationship with the entire partner:

- **Emerging**: There is no relationship, per se. The relationship is only beginning, and we barely know each other at the business level.

- **Transactional**: The level of trust is low. Most of the interactions between IT and the business unit revolve around specific requests.

- **Value-added:** The level of trust is climbing as the business unit realizes the value that IT brings to solving its problems.

- **Strategic partner**: The highest level of trust. IT is part of the client's team, providing advice and assistance.

For example, you might have a strong partner relationship with the VP of sales, but little to no relationship with anyone else in the sales department. This puts you in a difficult situation because all of your feedback and direction comes from one person, who may or may not have the entire story. It also means that, if that person leaves, you must build a new relationship from scratch.

Role expectations

Stakeholders also have different expectations of IT's role. Some might want IT to act as a Butler, doing everything it is asked to. Others might want IT to provide direction, like a Nanny.

The confusing part is that these people might belong to the same partner.

We talked about the importance of alignment, which also happens within the partner's stakeholders. If the decision-maker wants an Accountant, it will be difficult to be anything else even if the influencers want an Agent.

Understanding the role expectations of stakeholders also helps define how we should interact with them.

The different roles are:

Roles	
Accountant	Focus on cost control
Butler	Focus on delivering great service
Nanny	Take the lead role in providing direction
Agent	Play the role of a strategic partner

Defining priorities

"The business doesn't have any strategy!" If there is one thing I hear all the time from IT leaders, it's this. And, every single time, they are wrong. What they should say instead is, "The business doesn't have any strategy that we know of!"

That's right—just because a business doesn't have a strategy document doesn't mean that it lacks a strategy. Chances are, its business leaders clearly visualize where they are going and how to get there. But this vision might vary from one business unit to another.

Types of priorities

Priorities come in various forms and flavors. To make sense of them, we like to classify them into six different groups:

- **Regulatory**: The partner has no choice but to do these. It might be a new government regulation (a new tax rate coming into effect) or a corporate directive. In any case, there are no short-term benefits to expect; they need to get done.

- **Increase productivity**: This is one of the most popular priorities nowadays. It seems all business units are living with budget cuts or the need to absorb growth within their current budget. A lot of their priorities aim to do more with less, which can come from new business processes, new IT tools, or by letting go of old practices.

- **Increase sales**: This priority is popular with the sales business unit or with a region.

- **Reduce costs**: Similar to productivity, it aims at reducing real-cost items. This can include reducing the cost of raw materials or professional services or letting people go.

- **Program/mission**: These priorities are related directly to the mission of the organization. They are typically popular in the public sector and nonprofits.

- **Other**: This includes everything that doesn't fall into the previous categories.

Why is it important to categorize priorities? It gives a general sense of what is driving the organization on a day-to-day basis. An organization that focuses on increasing sales will not concern itself with reducing costs. Instead, it will prefer to put all its attention on business development. Thus, coming in with an idea to reduce cost would not be high on its radar. Likewise, talking about growth opportunity with someone struggling to increase productivity will be useless. They are focused on trying to survive day-to-day. Second, it allows you to see how different this partner is from the rest of the organization. While the organization is reducing costs, IT might be trying to deal with the increase in workload. The organization might be focusing on productivity, while marketing is concentrating on generating awareness for a new product or service.

Understanding how each partner differs from the rest of the organization helps you understand their priorities.

Identifying projects

Projects are the IT initiatives that make an impact on the business units. You probably already have many projects on the go, each designed for a specific business unit or to impact a department. Each project can potentially contribute to the department's priorities.

We can assign projects to the same five categories we use for priorities:

- **Regulatory**: The partner or organization doesn't have a choice. Business constraints (laws, regulations) or technology constraints (security, obsolescence) make this project mandatory.

- **Increase productivity**: These projects improve the productivity of the employees.

- **Increase sales**: These projects increase revenues.

- **Reduce costs**: These projects reduce the cost of raw materials, resources, or overhead (including human resources).

- **Program/mission:** These projects have priorities related directly to the mission of the organization. They are typically popular in the public sector and nonprofits.

- **Other**: These projects involve everything that doesn't fall into a previous category.

This categorization allows us to see our projects' and our entire portfolio's areas of impact. If 95 percent of the projects center around productivity, but most of the organization's priorities center on increasing revenue, we can see an obvious disconnect.

The second categorization consists of defining which specific priorities each project supports. Projects can support not only several priorities but different business units' priorities as well. For example, a new CRM can help the sales business unit increase the productivity of its representatives, track profitability by customer, and aid customer service in increasing customer satisfaction.

Together, this categorization can help us manage our project portfolio to provide the maximum benefit to the organization. This enables us to identify areas of neglect or overspending.

Measuring partnerships

A key theme of this book is the need to measure something to make sure it gets done. Partnerships are no exception. We will use the previous information to calculate the following indices.

The index we employ in our partnership management system is a little more complex, using more information and sophisticated models to calculate the Business Value Index. But, for the purpose of this book, we simplified the Business Value Index so that it is easy to calculate on the fly. These indicators are not perfect—far from it. But we've found, time and again, that they are good approximations of the business unit leaders' perceptions of value:

Metrics	Definition	Calculation
User Satisfaction Index	Uses a variation of the Net Promoter Score, a key indicator widely used by the business with their customers and clients	Percentage of users satisfied or very satisfied—Percentage of users dissatisfied or very dissatisfied
Relationship Index	Measures the number of stakeholders with a relationship level of at least 3. Value added. Ideally, each business unit would have at least 3.	0.30 points by stakeholders with a relationship status of at least 3, maxes at 1.00
Project Alignment Index	Provides a ratio of the priorities being actively supported by IT. It also gives a sense of just how important IT is to their future.	Percentage of priorities supported by at least one project
Simplified Business Value Index	The Business Value Index is the product of all three previous indices. It provides a general sense of the value IT provides to the department.	User Satisfaction Index * Relationship Index * Project Alignment Index

But do they provide an overall indication of the status of the relationship? For example, an IT team with no projects underway for a specific business unit is important but only as a provider of the Basics. It doesn't play a strategic role; thus, the score will be very low. On the other hand, an IT department that has several projects supporting departmental priorities might rate high on the Project Alignment Index, but if users are not satisfied, it will rate equally low on the Simplified Business Value Index. The indices are not cumulative; they are multiplicative. If any of the metrics is close to zero, then the overall Business Value Index is close to zero.

Example: Logistics department

Let's build a partnership plan together. The logistics department of BigCorp Inc. is a traditional transportation group that is trying to reinvent itself. For the longest time, it focused on optimizing its assets (trucks) so that they wouldn't run empty. Any time a truck drove without a full load meant money left on the table, literally.

In the past years, BigCorp has focused on being more customer-centric. It now proposes deliveries at its client's preference. If BigCorp committed to delivering a client's equipment on Tuesday at eleven o'clock, then you could bet that it would do so. The big retailers, which have strict delivery windows and huge penalties for missing them, drove a part of this, of course.

This transformation, although successful, proved very costly to BigCorp. A number of trucks left with less than a full load, and considerable pressure rose to change this.

Bob Logistics, the VP of logistics, feels the pressure. Bob has a lot of experience in logistics and wants to transform his business unit. Working for him are Cindy Planning, who is responsible for optimizing routes, and Mark, who is responsible for maintenance. IT already has a pretty good relationship with Bob but no real relationship with Cindy or Mark.

We already know enough to start building our partnership plan:

Stakeholders	Title	Priority	Relationship status
Bob Logistics	VP logistics	High	3. Value-added
Cindy Planning	Director route planning	High	1. Emergent
Mark Maintenance	Director maintenance	Standard	1. Emergent

Priorities	Stakeholders	Category	Projects
Improve asset utilization	Bob Logistics	Productivity	0
Reduce fuel consumption per stop	Cindy Planning Bob Logistics	Cost reduction	1
Reduce spare-parts inventory costs	Mark Maintenance	Cost reduction	1

We see that logistics is mostly preoccupied by cost reduction right now. The challenge, of course, is to accomplish this without having an impact on service. But this also tells us a few things: First, the corporate project to improve collaboration through a document-management system will probably not get a lot of attention right now because it doesn't align with any priorities. Second, Mark doesn't share the same priorities as his boss. Are Mark's initiatives lower in priority than Cindy's? Chances are, they are.

We also know that we have two projects being considered right now. One will put in place a system to optimize routes, and another will manage the spare-parts inventory. They are all in different stages of approval.

Projects	Stakeholders	Date submitted	Approval status
Route optimization system	Cindy Planning Bob Logistics	01/12/2014	Approved
Spare-parts inventory outsourcing	Mark Maintenance	12/10/2014	Evaluated

We're starting to get a pretty good picture of Bob's business unit. We understand the three main players, their priorities, and the projects they are working on. We also understand the relationship levels we have with them and recognize that Cindy will become an important player for us in the next year. Because we've been running user-satisfaction surveys for a few months, we have a pretty good idea of the satisfaction level. This allows us to calculate the Business Value Index.

USI (User Satisfaction Index)	RI (Relationship Index)	PAI (Project Alignment Index)	sBVI (Simplified Business Value Index)
0.65	0.30	0.66	**0.13**

This provides us with an overall Simplified Business Value Index (sBVI) of 13 percent. Not great. But we also see that simply by building a relationship with Cindy and Mark, we would be able to increase it to 39 percent. This makes sense, as it would give us a deeper set of relationships and put us less at risk if Bob were to leave.

Imperfect information

What happens when we know very little about our partner? We often face this situation in our workshops with our clients. We work through finance and HR, but the information gets a little lighter when talking about sales and goes blank when talking with operations, transportation, and such—to the point where we have a hard time identifying stakeholders, let alone priorities. But the reality is that we know more than we think. The information is distributed in many systems and people.

It is easy to gather information about how a client is using IT services today. One metric I like is the number of calls to the help-desk per user per month. This gives us a quick-and-dirty level of how much the organization depends on IT. Knowing that the industry average is around one call per user per month, anyone calling more might have issues with reliability or training, while anyone calling less might have given up on IT. Understanding how each partner varies from the organization as a whole helps determine who your users are and who they should be. Understanding which services employees use and how much also helps define what kind of users they are. Do they request more or fewer projects than the rest of the organization?

A second useful metric is user satisfaction. Are users more or less satisfied than the organization average? Do they feel their basic needs are being met? We often find business units that are consistently dissatisfied, simply because the services are not adapted to their needs. An engineering department calling less than the rest of the organization might find support weak. Its users prefer to support themselves and call the help-desk only when they have to. On the other hand, a finance group that calls the help-desk more than average will also be dissatisfied because they lack the skills or competencies to do basic operations.

Understanding these different realities helps define strategies to better serve users.

Step 2. Set objectives

As we begin to better understand all our partners, it becomes time to decide what we want to accomplish with them.

Some of my clients get confused when I talk about setting objectives with each business unit. Most of them reply something along the lines of "Aren't our objectives THEIR objectives? After all, aren't we there to serve them?"

Of course, our mission is to help the business units, but partnerships go both ways. The business units should be getting what they need from you to operate effectively, and you should be getting what you need from them to meet your own objectives.

Having clear objectives for each business unit helps align the IT team in its delivery. The project manager can keep someone in mind when deciding the next project; the help-desk manager can eliminate sources of frustration or costs.

Objectives

Type	Definition	Example of Objectives
Regulatory	The obligations IT needs to meet: Corporate systems security Data integrity	Reduce the number of users using non-authorized file-sharing programs
Productivity	Improve the productivity of IT personnel Reduce the amount of work to be performed	Reduce the number of calls to the help-desk from 1.6 per user per month to the organization average of 1.1 calls per user per month
Cost reduction	Reduce the use of IT resources	Reduce the number of user licenses for the corporate ERP system Reduce printing
Relationship	Develop or improve the level of the relationship with different stakeholders	Participate in business unit's monthly meeting
Other	Anything else that doesn't fall in the other categories	

Developing objectives

Objectives cannot be developed in isolation. It requires the participation of various parts of the IT department.

Using a partnership planning session is one of the easiest ways to accomplish this. We've found, with our clients, that it is the quickest way not only to update plans but also to keep the entire team in the loop.

We typically dedicate an hour every month to this activity, meeting with key IT leaders and relationship managers to update two to three plans. Of course, we assume the owner of the plan has done his or her homework ahead of time.

Throughout the session, we review the following:

- Stakeholders: Determine if there were any changes, both in the people and the status of the relationships.

- Priorities: Did any priorities change? Did any new ones come in?

- Projects: Were any new projects identified? Are any old projects no longer relevant?

- Objectives: What should our objectives and goals be? Did we meet them? Are they still relevant?

Example: Logistics (part II)

Let's keep building our partnership plan with our logistics example from BigCorp.

Now we're turning our attention to their usage of IT services. We looked at the user-satisfaction results for the past few months, and we found that the logistics department scores consistently lower than the rest of the organization.

A major issue seems to be related to equipment and connectivity, which makes a lot of sense. We know that drivers on the road often have little access to cellular connectivity, making it difficult to stay in touch and react to changes in routes, for example. But that's not all; we also see that office employees are complaining about their applications being slow and difficult to use. Route tracking and optimization systems take a lot of horsepower to constantly integrate all of the data and analyze them in real-time.

When we examine the number of tickets, we see that they are significantly lower than average. Although we expect that from the truck drivers, we see the same pattern for office employees. Is it a case of users having fewer problems than average, or did they simply give up on the help-desk? If we consider the satisfaction scores, they might have given up.

The IT leader and relationship manager are preoccupied by these results. If logistics is to install new systems and change the way the company works, it needs to make sure the users will respond positively to these changes. If IT lacks credibility, users will resist change and the project might fail. Logistics coordinators will return to their old paper planning methods and simply abandon the systems.

Thus, one of the team's first priorities is to improve the level of satisfaction with equipment and support. The project required replacing the equipment anyway, so perhaps we could go ahead and replace it ahead of time to boost satisfaction.

The second priority is to get people to use support. We first need to understand how they use support today (what kind of tickets they open) and the reason they don't call more. We also need to build a relationship with the truck drivers, as they've never been big users in the past. An awareness program that includes examples of when to call will help them understand support's role.

Finally, we also recognize that Cindy will play a major role.

Objectives	Category	Status
Develop relationship with Cindy Planning	Alignment	Not started
Improve timesheet utilization rate	Regulatory	Not started
Reduce last-minute computer replacement	Productivity	Not started
Reduce number of calls to the help-desk	Productivity	In progress

The team also started planning activities for itself. The first was to develop the partnership plan (which is now done), so it can close this activity. Activities tied to the objectives should also be part of this table, obviously, so they can be tracked.

Activity	Stakeholders	Type	Status
Investigate issue with slow route-planning tool	Cindy Planning	Task	Open
Review low driver satisfaction with IT equipment	Bob Logistics	Task	Open
Schedule a meeting with Bob Logistics regarding costs	Bob Logistics	Meeting	Open

We now have a complete partnership plan. The process to build the plan isn't long or difficult, but sometimes it requires information we simply don't have. This is why it's an interactive process.

Get the template

Get the template for partnership plans at:

GreenElephantTeam.com/BVIT

Step 3. Managing the relationship

Once we have established a plan, the real work starts. Now it's about evolving the plan, meeting objectives, and setting new ones. Stakeholders, priorities, and projects evolve, and the plan helps us adapt. The easiest way to manage the relationship is through a formal mechanism—a partnership-review meeting.

The partnership-review meeting

Any relationship suffers through different friction points. As the relationship evolves, it is easy to take each other for granted or assume that all parties have remained the same over the years. But the reality is different. People evolve. Where there was once trust can be doubt. Small issues or problems can become big. Communications can be misinterpreted.

Commercial account managers realized long ago that a relationship needs to have periodic review points. Such a meeting allows the account manager to reset the relationship, to address and resolve issues (if any), and to understand how the client is evolving. Without these periodic meetings, it would be easy to let the relationship deteriorate and become irrelevant.

We borrowed the concept of the quarterly review from these managers and adapted it to the context of an internal service provider. To make it seem less "sales-y," we are calling it the partnership review.

The partnership review has three main objectives:

- To demonstrate our credibility

- To remove dissatisfiers

- To promote alignment

Credibility

Our first objective is to demonstrate our credibility as a service provider. We do this by being totally transparent about our performance during the last period. Using performance indicators helps the partners see how your service evolves (is it getting better or worse?) and shows that you make the basic services a priority for your organization.

It is tempting to camouflage our bad performance and to justify issues or problems by blaming outside factors or partners. But this doesn't change the fact that, in the eyes of our partners, we are responsible. Thus, it is better to accept responsibility, even for things outside your control. After all, you are the one delivering the service.

We also demonstrate our credibility by showing that we did what we said we would do. Thoroughly reviewing all of the commitments we made, their status, and the next steps (if they are not closed) shows that we are dependable. It also serves to confirm that the issue is indeed solved.

Remove dissatisfiers

Our second objective is to remove dissatisfiers that may have crept up since the last meeting. Chances are, a small irritant may have appeared. It could be within the basic services themselves (the printer is giving trouble) or something more serious, such as the way a project is being managed.

Most likely, the partner wouldn't have bothered to open a ticket or call you because the issues seemed too trivial to justify the time. But trivial issues tend to accumulate and become major irritants. The relationship can die from a thousand tiny cuts.

Promote alignment

Our third objective is to promote alignment with the partner. By understanding or confirming their major priorities and constraints, IT can align its activities, projects, and choices in the direction that fits them best.

However, alignment simply won't happen if the partner remains unconvinced that you are worthy of its time. This is why the first few account reviews tend to focus on objectives 1 and 2. As the trust level improves, the partner opens up to discuss alignment.

The partnership-review agenda

We've developed and tested the following agenda with our clients over the last few years. To be successful, the partnership-review meeting needs to be short and to the point. No one wants to sit though pages and pages of statistics, charts, and whatnot. Ideally, the meeting should last no more than thirty minutes—at least the agenda part.

Partnership-review meeting agenda:

1. Operational performance: The performance of the services provided.
2. Service usage: How the client uses the services provided compared to other groups. Opportunities for improving service usage.
3. Focus and priorities: The projects that will be worked on as a priority for the next quarter.
4. Ongoing/new projects and major milestones.
5. Status and issues: Ongoing issues and their status from the previous account review.
6. Upcoming events: A summary of the events that will have an impact on the partner.

As the relationship grows, the partner will simply take the operational performance at face value and speed up through the first few points. The meetings frequently derail to talk about upcoming initiatives and business objectives, which is great. After all, this is why we hold the meeting in the first place. But the conversation shouldn't be allowed in that direction until the bases have been covered, even if done quickly.

Participants

The partnership review should be attended by the person in charge of the relationship from the IT side (the business relationship manager, IT leader, or equivalent), the principal stakeholder from the client side, and one or two of his or her colleagues.

It can be tempting to involve the project managers, the IT service managers, the business analyst, and whatnot. Although it would help keep everyone around the table on the same page, it would also defeat the purpose: building a relationship.

Additionally, the conversation might derail to more operational issues, such as project issues. Keeping the group tight will help focus the discussion, shorten the meeting, and ensure that no one cancels it in the future.

Frequency

We recommend holding quarterly meetings. Any more, and we quickly run out of subjects to discuss, a surefire way to make certain that stakeholders cancel the meeting at the last minute. Holding meetings further apart leads to a loss of relevance; issues are long-gone by the time our meeting occurs. Quarterly appears to be the sweet spot for most of our clients.

But we should not wait until the next meeting to address issues. In fact, the quarterly meeting should bring nothing new to the table. It should simply recap the situation. Any issues, problems, or operational failures should be communicated as they happen. Therefore, we would expect to communicate much more frequently than simply during the quarterly partnership-review meeting.

Partnership review template and example

Having a supporting document always makes the meeting easier. But, in this case, less is more. We recommend keeping it to six pages (one per agenda item).

Get the template

Get the template for partnership reviews at:

GreenElephantTeam.com/BVIT

Frequent issues

While working with our clients, I identified the major issues that arise when conducting partnership reviews.

Scheduling the meeting

The first step of the partnership review is to actually plan to meet with the person in charge. In the beginning of the relationship, we often see business stakeholders delegating the meeting to others, canceling at the last minute ("something came up—let's do it some other time"), or simply declining the meeting.

Obviously, this is the first (and big) sign that the business stakeholder sees no value in meeting with you. He or she doesn't believe that IT can benefit the organization—or, at least, it is not worth the time.

A few strategies that work well include sending a quick resume of what the meeting would have covered. It needs to be a few sentences, tops, or else the stakeholder will simply not read it. Here is an example:

"Hi, John. I understand you are too busy for a meeting right now. Let me give you the condensed version:

- IT service performance was at 97 percent for the last quarter, up two points.
- Your business unit logs twice as many requests for support as the rest of the organization. We'll work with your staff to see what's behind this. I'll update you at our next quarterly meeting.
- Your top three projects are still green. We don't expect any issues. Give me a call if you'd like to discuss any of this."

No one likes to be different. Knowing that his business unit uses the help-desk twice as much will probably raise his curiosity—perhaps enough to get you a meeting next time.

Incredulity toward performance metrics

"Ninety-seven percent performance, yeah right! The system is down almost daily!"

Business executives get most of their information about IT performance from their own staff. If a metric conflicts with their perception of the service, then cognitive dissonance will happen, and they will simply reject the metric.

This is why it is very important for the metric to accurately represent the reality FOR THE USER. Mentioning that the servers had a 99.999 percent availability means little to the user—especially if the network went down daily.

Additionally, IT is used for many excuses: "My presentation isn't ready because the system was slow." "My computer crashed and I couldn't finish the TPS report." It is the business equivalent of "the dog ate my homework." Unfortunately, it is still very prevalent.

How can someone work through this misconception? Simply by owning up to it. "You don't seem to agree with the performance metric. Is there something I'm not aware of?" Volunteer to talk to the employees who said the network was down or that the systems were not working. Take every complaint very seriously. Follow-up with both the employees and the stakeholder.

If every complaint gets investigated, employees will probably stop using IT as an excuse. At the very least, it shows that you stand behind your numbers.

Refusing to share priorities

Some stakeholders might be willing to talk about IT's performance but clam up when it's time to talk about their priorities. They might be evasive, noncommittal, or simply closed to the subject.

The message is clear: they simply don't trust you with that information.

Building the kind of trust that convinces stakeholders to share takes time. The idea is not to abandon them along the way. It might take several months, if not years, before they open up about their priorities.

But what if you need them in the meantime?

Using the five different classifications of priorities (regulatory, cost reduction, productivity, sales increase, and other), we can simply ask them which of the five best represents their main priority—and leave it at that. Even then, they might not be willing to share. That's fine. Respecting their need for privacy will help to build trust.

Talking behind your back

Some stakeholders might act as if everything is going great between their business unit and IT and then afterward simply tell everyone who wants to listen how IT is not doing its job.

Being a partner doesn't mean being a carpet. It is okay to bring up the issue.

Simply say something like, "I've heard through the grapevines that you were not satisfied with our services. Can we talk about that? It's hard for us to change if we're not aware of the issue."

Having the courage to bring up the matter will show that you are not simply a provider but a partner. And, as such, you expect them to complain to you, not to others. It also demonstrates that you won't shy away from the difficult issues, even if the issue is them. Being able to address these concerns respectfully, but firmly, will help build the partnership over time. And it will prevent false rumors in the short-term.

Regardless of the obstacle, the key is persistence. Think of the relationship you have with your best suppliers. Chances are that it wasn't always easy. Perhaps you even refused to take his or her calls at the beginning, not understanding what this person could do for you. But his or her persistence paid off, not only for the supplier but for you, as well. Being persistent (politely) will show that you are in this for the long-term.

5. Fewer but better

Do you trust your team?

An important meeting just came up. You are to make a presentation on the biggest priorities in IT for the coming year. The executives will be present and will ask questions. There's only one problem: you will be on vacation that day. What are you going to do?

Your boss, aware that you made your plans months in advance, proposes you send someone else from your team. After all, it is only a presentation. What could go wrong?

At this point, you have an important decision to make: do you cancel your plans so you can make the presentation, or do you delegate?

If you're like 73 percent of the CIOs we surveyed, you will find a way to give the presentation yourself. You will interrupt or cancel your plans if need be. Not because you crave being in front of an audience—no, because you don't have enough trust in anyone else on your team.

A surprising number of CIOs don't trust their team for anything that doesn't concern technology. They'd prefer their team to avoid talking with the business. They don't trust them to possess the relationship skills or the situational awareness required for intelligent discussions.

In fact, when we dig further, we find that many CIOs are dissatisfied with the composition of their team. Given the choice, they would replace a fair number of them—but they don't because they feel their hands are tied. They most likely inherited the current team and feel that letting one go would cause issues, such as losing an understanding of the systems or the infrastructure.

So, they tolerate them. And, budgets being tight, they assign them roles that may be inappropriate for their level of competency.

One question I like to ask IT leaders is, "Who's next in line to take your job?" It often leads to the same response: "You know, I don't think there is anyone in the team ready yet to take on this job."

I find this interesting for two reasons. First, it shows a critical issue in the organization. After all, if no one is ready to take on the job, chances are the IT leader is failing at grooming a successor.

Second, it shows that IT leaders have poor expectations of their team. Most IT leaders underestimate their team members' capabilities.

How Level 4 IT departments manage their teams

Level 4 IT departments manage their teams in three ways:

1. They don't tolerate problem employees.
2. They focus on quality over quantity.
3. They coach their team members.

1. **Problem employees**

I was discussing this specific subject with Jean, the CIO of an energy company. He complained that one of his key technical people was good with computers but had a tendency to infuriate users—to the point where several of them no longer wanted to work with him anymore. Unfortunately, this individual held almost all the corporate memory of their custom applications. And, because these applications were so specific to their organization, Jean feared no one else could step in.

Jean faced a serious conundrum: what could he do with this individual? His first instinct was to hide him from the business, to isolate him and let other people act as a liaison.

But this strategy had a serious flaw: it gave the message to everyone that it is okay to be inadequate.

Talking with Jean, I wondered if it might be too late to influence this person's behavior. The organization had tolerated his attitude for years and had even promoted him because of his technical expertise.

The same story with a Level 4

I met Sylvain, the CIO of a transportation organization, a few years ago. His organization is a great example of a Level 4 IT department. He builds strong relationships with the business and provides great project delivery and exceptional support.

Sylvain had a serious issue. One of his team members was not performing at par, getting into issues with the business. This individual had a strong sense of how things should be done and was not receptive to different points of view. He remained convinced that he knew better than anyone in the organization and, as such, didn't feel like he needed to involve the business.

Sylvain discussed the issue with the individual immediately upon hearing of it. He gave him some coaching and defined a plan to correct the situation. One month later, the same situation happened. Nothing had changed. Sylvain terminated his contract.

The big difference lay in the fact that the individual wasn't a team member just yet. He had been hired as a contractor for a specific project. This contract served as a way to evaluate the performance and the fit of the individual before making a hiring decision.

Sylvain is picky about the people he hires. He not only hires people with great skills, but also finds employees that could potentially take over his job. He wants great team members, great relationship people, and great leaders. Even for technical positions.

This has given Sylvain a team of focused, talented individuals. It also lets Sylvain go on vacation any time he pleases, knowing that he can rely 100 percent on his team.

Dealing with problem employees

Problem employees can have severe consequences on the relationship with the business and on the team. Nothing is more destructive to collaboration than having to deal with someone who is difficult. Most people will simply ignore the problem and work on their own instead. In just a few months, this situation can destroy a team that took years to build and motivate.

But firing people is not always a practical option. First, it isn't that easy to let someone go. It is a difficult process that can take months—and it is rarely necessary.

A better option is to bring people back in.

Most problem employees are people that fall into one of three categories:

Problem 1: They don't have the skills/knowledge.

I've never run into a situation in which employees were underperforming on purpose. No one gets up in the morning to do a poor job. We all take pride in what we do and like to be recognized for it, but problems arise when employees lack the skills to do their job.

This often happens in IT departments, where people have been hired for their technical expertise. However, promotion after promotion has left them in charge of managing people, and they find themselves under-skilled. They become low performers where they once were a superstar, something that's difficult to accept for anybody.

Level 4 IT departments recognize that, as the position changes, so do the job requirements and the skills required. Promoting someone into a management position without providing management training is asking for trouble. A proactive training plan can help resolve many of these issues. A reactive training plan is also a good option, providing a chance for the person to regain the level of proficiency required.

Problem 2: They don't understand the expectations.

A programmer's or analyst's job description is pretty straightforward. But, when we look at managers, project managers, and business relationship managers, it quickly becomes fuzzy, at best.

The expectations for various positions are not always clearly documented, leaving a significant gap between what people think their role is versus what their managers think. A project manager might happily manage the schedule and paperwork associated with the project while his or her manager expects him or her to make it successful, whatever it takes.

It is the supervisor's job to clarify expectations, something that Level 4 IT departments do not only once, but continually. Managers regularly meet with employees to discuss their performance and coach them by revisiting the expectations for their role.

Problem 3: They are not motivated to perform.

Managers come and go in organizations. Rarely does an IT leader stay on for more than four years these days. Thus, career employees will go through a major leadership change every couple of years. They will have a new supervisor, a new IT leader, or a new business leader. Each one brings various promises of "100 day plans," "new strategic vision," and "change of culture." It's easy for these employees to see these changes as fads and simply "wait them out," especially when the undertone of the messages is that they are part of the problem.

Motivating people to perform requires us to bring them along with us, not leave them on the sidelines or blame them for the current situation. They controlled the situation no more in the past than they do today. Blaming them for something they probably didn't agree with in the first place helps no one.

Level 4 IT departments build motivation by involving everyone in the picture. Instead of blaming the past, they talk about "evolution" and "progression." They spend a considerable amount of time communicating their vision, not only through words but though actions.

An IT leader who talks about the importance of customer service but never visits the help-desk will have little credibility.

2. Fewer people, better paid and better equipped

We still tend to look at productivity in terms of manual labor. If one employee can produce ten widgets a day, then two employees will produce twenty. It's simple arithmetic. If one is good, two is better.

This thinking still drives a lot of today's hiring decisions. If all project managers are equal, let's take the cheapest one we can find.

This will help us stretch our budget and allow us to hire even more people.

This thinking no longer holds true when dealing with knowledge workers. Productivity varies widely between individuals. A top performer might be twice as productive as a good performer. And, in terms of business impact, that is an order of magnitude higher.

Competencies like teamwork, collaboration, and leadership become critical—and these are the competencies that really make a difference in knowledge work.

Level 4 IT departments recognize this and build their team accordingly. They focus on hiring top talent, people with not only the expertise for the job today, but with excellent potential for the future. They also provide their employees with the right learning opportunities (formal and informal) to continually develop.

Level 4 IT departments would rather spend 20 percent to 25 percent more to hire a top performer than hire more people. They understand that fewer, but better, will have a greater impact.

Hiring right

The easiest way to avoid problem employees is to forgo hiring them in the first place. This is why Level 4 IT departments have very stringent hiring processes. They prefer to "test" new employees through a contract or a project before making a final hiring decision. Once someone has been hired, it becomes considerably more difficult to deal with the problem. However, this makes the hiring process much more arduous for both the IT leaders and the person being hired.

Hiring often comes as a crisis. Budgets being tight, IT departments don't have the luxury of having superfluous people on a day-to-day basis. We often make hiring decisions quickly, lacking the time to interview dozens of candidates.

The hiring process also considers that the person will be working as part of a team. Departments must ensure the person's personality and work ethics will fit with the other team members so that the team will remain cohesive. This doesn't mean they always hire the same profile. A little dissension is always a good thing, after all. But team cohesion makes sure that, at the end of the day, the team will be able to rally and move forward.

Competencies

Most hiring decisions are based on technical skills. Can the person program in C#? Are they project management professional (PMP) certified? Technical skills are important, but rarely predict success.

Level 4 IT departments look at three different sets of competencies:

Competency 1. Technical

Does the person have the technical skills required for his or her position? This is the typical criteria for hiring and probably represents 75 percent of the job postings today.

Technical skills requirements represent a mastery of the tools, but they often fail to include other elements, such as the ability to understand the bigger picture, to understand what's coming next, or to see the impact of what is done on other systems. A system administrator who doesn't understand the impact that cloud-based solutions will have on the business in the next five years will quickly become a liability.

Competency 2. Business

Does the person understand the business context of the organization? How the organization makes money? Or how it delivers its mission? Does this person understand the context and challenges in doing so?

IT doesn't work in isolation. Few people enjoy the luxury of having to perform only their job without understanding the bigger context.

Level 4 IT departments consider business competencies to be just as important as technical skills. IT needs to understand the bigger context of what they do to have an impact and have educated discussions with the business. All of this can happen only if the IT department actually lives in the organization and understands it.

Level 4 IT departments go as far as having their team do rotations in the business, from a few hours to a few weeks. This allows the team to understand the real context.

Business competencies make the difference between a simple supplier and an IT department deeply integrated within the business.

Competency 3. Behavioral

Behavioral competencies, often the most difficult to assess, are the most critical.

These competencies include the ways a person interacts with others, conducts negotiations, comes to agreements, and meets short-term objectives, along with the long-term ones. Can this person deliver a difficult project and maintain good relationships, for example?

Behavioral competencies make the difference between an IT department that pushes solutions and one that works collaboratively and as a partner.

Ongoing evolution

Of course, no one possesses all three sets of competencies when hired. Expecting new hires to understand the business is unreasonable. This is why Level 4 IT departments use competency assessments not only for new hires, but for everyone. By mapping the competency requirements, Level 4 IT departments can identify gaps and train or coach their teams appropriately. This also helps to set expectations of the team members.

Equipment

You spend time and money hiring the best race-car drivers you can find. You now have a great team. Would you give them minivans to drive? Of course not—top performers need top tools.

I was talking to a technical person as he struggled to make a diagram in Power Point. He kept rearranging all the boxes and trying make them fit on a page. I asked him why he wasn't using Microsoft Visio to do his work (or any other diagramming tool on the market). His response was simple: "We don't have enough licenses for it."

Looking on the Internet, I found that the consumer price of Visio is $356. I think we all agree that IT departments pay much less for it as part of their value license. Yet, this was a fairly senior individual, probably paid $100 to $125 per hour to struggle with poor software because the company didn't want to invest another $356.

I have dozens of examples like that. Most IT professionals have very little margin to buy what they need in their day-to-day work. They must go through approbation levels and forms to justify even the smallest of expenses. What if a web app could help them right away with one of their projects? Nope, they need approval. What if they can purchase an add-on instead of coding everything from scratch? Nope, it's easier to simply spend the time on it.

Level 4 IT departments understand this well. They go out of their way to give the right equipment to their team members. They also make it easy for them to get what they need, quickly. This small increase in expenditures is repaid ten-fold by the increase in productivity and value-added work.

3. Coaching the team

Constant cost optimization has left IT in a difficult situation. Most IT leaders work over seventy hours a week. Projects and operations are understaffed and overstretched. It comes as no surprise, therefore, that IT leaders have started doing more and more of the work themselves. We often see IT leaders managing projects, resolving operational crises, negotiating with vendors, and smoothing relations with the business.

This leaves very little time for team managers to actually manage their staff. In fact, according to our survey, most IT professionals see their manager less than one hour a week—and this time is typically spent working on crises.

When we consider that the ideal amount of time an employee needs to spend with their managers per week is six hours, we see that we fall very short of that, leaving employees in a situation in which they are unmanaged. It is difficult for them to have any face time with their managers to ask for feedback, advice, or orientation.

In an era in which employee engagement is critical, we actually do the opposite. They are left to themselves, expected to know what they have to do, and spend time with their managers only when something goes horribly wrong.

Level 4 IT departments take management very seriously. Most managers spend three to five hours per week with each employee in both formal and informal settings. In fact, Level 4 IT managers rarely have more than seven employees responding to them.

This ratio helps them spend more time with each employee and coach them effectively.

Becoming Level 4: Fewer but better

In an ideal world, you would be able to build your team from scratch. You would pick the best person for each role and train them to the necessary level. You would set up a selection process to weed out anyone who wouldn't fit in with the team and would slow the others down. You would build a team no one has ever seen before.

But you can't. You already have a team. You can't fire everyone and start over again. There are legacy systems only a handful of people understand, you have budget constraints, and it wouldn't look good with HR. So, what can you do?

We will look at how you can take your staff and realign them into a Level 4 IT department-worthy team.

Aligning the team

Employee alignment has three distinct, but essential components:

- Ability: Do employees have the right skills and competencies to use the system?

- Opportunity: Do employees have access to the equipment, do they have the correct tools, and do they have time to use the system?

- Motivation: What will the employees gain from using the system?

Only when all three elements come together are employees aligned.

1. Ability

Does your team have the competencies needed to do their job?

IT's role has evolved, and technical competencies alone no longer work. IT teams need a combination of technical, business, and behavioral skills to succeed. But a surprisingly high number of hiring decisions are still based on technical competencies only. Not convinced? Take a look at any employment board today. Search for any IT position, and you'll find that the vast majority of the job ad focuses on technical competencies. You might see something like, "Must have great communication skills," but nothing else provides further clarification. Are we talking about being able to communicate within the team? With clients? Or to make presentations?

Even technical competencies tend to focus on specific technologies and not on transposable competencies. For example, "Knowledge of C#" versus "Ability to develop an understanding of current systems and technologies." So, what competencies should we be looking at?

Technical:

- Design and develop applications and solutions.
- Understand existing systems and technology.
- Apply procedures, tools, and methods.

Business:

- Understand the business's organization, politics, and culture.
- Manage change in the business from IT applications.
- Further customer service.

Behavioral:

- Lead, inspire, and build trust.
- Build relationships and foster teamwork.
- Resolve conflicts and problems.

Evaluating competencies

We propose you do a quick evaluation of the competency level and the level of trust you feel toward each of your direct reports. You can even evaluate the level underneath if you have enough information. To keep things simple, we propose you use a three-point scale:

Competency rating	
1	Severely under expectations
2	Somewhat below expectations
3	Meet or exceed expectations

This diagnostic should take you less than one minute per employee. If you don't know how to evaluate someone, I would suggest you leave it blank. The employee may simply never have had the opportunity to demonstrate this competency. Then, calculate the total score of all nine competencies.

Competencies	Employee		
	1	**2**	**3**
Technical			
Ability to design and develop applications and solutions			
Ability to understand existing systems and technology			
Ability to apply procedures, tools, and methods			
Business			
Understanding business organization, politics, and culture			
Managing change in the business from IT applications			
Customer service			
Behavioral			
Leading, inspiring, and building trust			
Building relationships/teamwork			
Resolving conflicts and problems			
Total			

Ideally, each employee should rate a 24 or above, meeting most of your expectations with regard to technical, business, and behavioral competencies, with some room for improvement. An employee below 21 would need some pretty serious coaching; he or she is not fit for the job and must be brought up to par as quickly as possible.

An employee below 18 is another issue altogether. This is a hiring mistake. The employee is clearly not suited for the task at hand. He or she falls below your expectations in almost every category and is clearly unsuitable for the position. How did this employee get there in the first place? Perhaps your expectations for the position changed or someone else hired this employee? Perhaps the position evolved? In either case, this person is a liability to your team. His or her lack of competency probably reflects poor work in other areas and is visible to colleagues. An underperforming team member forces everyone else to work that much harder, creating resentment.

Users and business leaders notice this, too, and it makes them wonder what kind of operation you are running. How can you tolerate this level of performance? It goes a long way in creating credibility issues.

Unfortunately, you have little choice when it comes to severely underperforming team members: you have to let them go. They are a drag on your team and a liability to your credibility.

But what if several team members are low?
What if you have several team members who score very low? Perhaps you are a new leader coming in with a team already in place. You didn't get to choose any of them. After the evaluation, you see that they are all ill-suited for their roles. You cannot let everyone go; it would just create havoc. Then the question becomes: are your expectations realistic?

Training
When I talk with IT leaders, I'm always surprised to see how detached they are from their staff's training curriculum. Most IT employees decide for themselves what kind of training they need every year. They are often given a budget and told to find something that suits their needs.

This approach is great in theory because it puts the ownership of self-development back where it belongs: on the employee—but in practice, not so much. We find that people tend to overspecialize in their area. They go for the training and certification to reach the next level of their specialty, without real concern about whether it is required. In the meantime, they might be missing out on other competencies that would make a real difference.

We've already seen that customer service skills are twice as important as technical skills for user satisfaction. Yet, how many hours of customer-service training did your staff receive last year? If you're like most IT leaders, none.

Your training plan should start from the evaluation you just completed. If a vast majority of your team scored low on customer service, then it makes sense to focus training in this area. If gaps vary, then assign priorities for each team member. This doesn't mean they cannot decide their own training, but part of it should be directed to meet your goals.

Tools

The amount of time that is wasted simply because people are not using the right tools is incredible. They either don't know that such a tool exists, or they cannot get it. In the corporate world, it is often the second one. Salaries are fixed and will be paid, no matter what. Tools, on the other hand, come from a different budget that we try to reduce as much as possible. Thus, if someone wants to save a few hours by spending a few hundred dollars, our reflex is to simply say no. Buying something is very difficult. You need purchase orders, authorizations, etc. Spending the extra time is the easiest solution. It's also the worst.

When we do this, we teach our employees to discount their time. They could be making something that has an impact on the organization, but they are stuck spending hours to save a few dollars. Time is precious, especially if you have few people. Investing in the right tools makes a lot of sense.

The best basketball players won't get a chance to show their skills if they never get court time. Having the ability to do the work is the first step. Receiving the actual opportunity to do the work is the second.

2. Opportunity

The second component of alignment is opportunity. Your team members might have the skills to do their work, but are they given the chance to do it?

We find, over and over again, that team members are not lacking ability, but opportunity. Either team members are never in a position to highlight their skills, or the current environment discourages them from applying those skills in the first place.

Trust and opportunities

Earlier, we looked at the role of trust in building relationships with business units. The same principle applies to your team members. Without trust, it is very difficult to build and maintain a relationship. So the question is: do you trust your team members?

When it comes to many employee performance problems, the level of trust between the employee and the manager is to blame. The manager doesn't trust the employee to make decisions alone; thus, he or she spends too much time micromanaging or isolating the employee, leading to dissatisfaction and disengagement. Employees resent the situation, and performance goes down as they do the bare minimum to get by. Obviously, this is not an employee we want as part of the team.

For employees to accept responsibilities, you need to trust that they will not only be able to face challenges but will also make the right decisions along the way. If you don't trust them to be alone in front of a stakeholder while representing IT, you will find it impossible to delegate anything of substance to them.

For each employee, I propose you measure the level of trust:

1. Low: I wouldn't leave this person alone with a box of matches.

2. Average: I would leave on vacation but would check in from time to time.

3. High: I would hand them the keys to my car.

How many of your employees do you trust with your car? If it's less than 50 percent, you have a serious problem.

A team needs a high level of trust to be effective. As an IT leader, it is important to be able to delegate and then move on to something else. Sixty-one percent of IT leaders today complain that they have too much to do, that they have no time to actually manage. But, when we look at their workloads, we see that they take on responsibilities and tasks that their team should be doing. Why? They don't trust their team to successfully complete these tasks, so they'd rather do them themselves.

Building trust

If you are like many of my clients, you've just finished this exercise, and you are surprised and worried to find so few people on your team that you actually trust. Most need some level of scrutiny, in your opinion. So, what is the solution—fire everybody?

You can actually build trust with your team the same way you do with your stakeholders by having them meet small commitments. Minor tasks, activities, or projects are great ways to prove to yourself, and to them, that they can take on responsibilities and deliver. Have them run meetings with stakeholders, so you can see them in action. Of course, there will be issues along the way. Some things will fall apart, and they will make mistakes. But that's where you can help them and coach them to greater levels of performance.

At the end of this process, if you find that you still don't trust everyone on your team, then unfortunately you need to think hard about whether there is a place for them. If you cannot depend on your team, you will always be tempted to do their jobs, and you won't have time to do yours.

Metrics

The other factor that removes the opportunity to deliver great value is metrics. We've said over and over again that what gets measured gets done. Unfortunately, we tend to measure what is easy to measure, not what is important.

For example, it is easy to measure the number of calls a help-desk agent closes per day. Ideally, we should measure the number of closed calls in which the user was happy and the problem did not reappear, but that's much more difficult to do. So, instead, we measure what is easy; thus, the incentive to close calls is much higher than the incentive to satisfy users. As an agent, I could leave a ticket open until tomorrow, so I can follow-up with the user, but that would negatively impact my numbers.

Metrics drive behavior, good or bad. If our metrics go against the behavior we are trying to promote, then it is best to disregard or even remove them.

Your team has the skills and the opportunity. Now how do you get them to actually do the work?

3. Motivation

If ability is the wheels and opportunity is the road, then motivation is the engine. It is what separates people who meet expectations from those who exceed them.

But being motivated is one thing—being motivated about the right things is another. We usually don't have problems getting an IT team to focus on a new project or initiative. Everyone is excited at the idea of installing new software or hardware. But motivating a team to follow processes, to answer calls from users, and to build relationships with the business is another story.

Changing behavior

We will start with one key assumption: everyone in your team wants to do a good job. It is very rare that we see an IT professional who wants to take it easy or do the bare minimum. Most IT professionals don't get up in the morning to annoy people and perform poorly. They want to do a good job and be recognized for it.

The real problem is not willingness but time. IT professionals are solicited from everywhere. They have plenty of conflicting priorities, and it is easy for them to work all day simply responding to requests. How do they make the time to work on what's important?

Covey provided an excellent categorization of activities based on two criteria: urgency and importance. Most people spend their day working on the important-urgent tasks. A report is due tomorrow, a request came in for a change, a system is down, etc. To some extent, we also work on the nonimportant-urgent tasks as well. Urgency is an appealing driver; we want to make sure we don't drop the ball on anything. An urgent task, even if not important, becomes quickly visible when it remains unfinished.

And then, there are the important-nonurgent tasks: the tasks we should be doing but seldom have time to do. A lot of the tasks we discuss in this book fall into this category. Doing them will add value, but nothing will catch fire if we don't do them today. As the saying goes, "Tomorrow is always the busiest day of the week." So, how can we, as IT leaders, get the important-nonurgent tasks completed? Easy—we make them urgent.

What gets measured gets done

One of the easiest ways to make a task urgent is through monthly Key Performance Indicators (KPI). The simple fact of measuring systematically, every month, forces everyone to at least think about performance. Because no one likes to see their KPI go down (or at least, not go up), it brings a new level of attention to the matter.

This is the strategy we use with our clients to drive changes in behaviors. Using monthly satisfaction surveys, we can bring the importance of user satisfaction to the same level as budgets or availability metrics.

But does it make sense to measure without a strategy?

"We don't have the time for a user satisfaction program right now. What's the point of measuring?" You probably don't have a clear plan to meet your budget, either, yet you still measure it. If it's important to you, you want to know where you stand. You want to know if it is under control or if you need to implement a new plan. Those who accept being kept in the dark send the message that satisfaction is simply not important to them.

Transformation program

"We're going through a transformation program right now. We'll start measuring when we're stable." No, you won't. If you don't plan on measuring when it counts the most, you won't measure later.

IT departments going through a transformation program need a way to anchor themselves in reality and measure their results. Transforming without understanding the results is like driving blindfolded. We might cover a lot of mileage, but we don't know if we're headed in the right direction. And we might hit a wall.

Communication

Another key to motivation is frequent communication with the entire team/department. It is easy to talk about user satisfaction and value when you navigate in this environment all day long. But when your job is to fix systems or manage technology, it can be difficult to understand exactly what is meant by all this. "How does it affect my job?"

I once had a manager at IBM who told our department that we needed to "think outside the box." He left it at that, and no one really understood what he meant. Conceptually, we understood that we needed to find new methods of doing things, which was fine—but were we to disregard current processes? Were we to reinvent our tools? What kind of latitude did we have to think outside the box? How big was the box? Without some concrete examples, it is difficult for people to visualize these concepts.

When is the last time you talked to your entire team? Perhaps your team is too big to talk to everyone at once, fine. So, when is the last time you went around and tried to talk to all of your groups? And did you provide examples of what you mean with each of your orientations?

Most communications from IT leaders tend to be regulatory: you must do this process for this reason. "Fill in your timesheet before Friday." "Fill in the employee 360."

But what if you were to meet with your team or send a video once a month, giving an example of someone who executed your vision particularly well?

Increasing your level of communication and involvement with the team will help clarify the vision for all employees, give them a chance to ask questions and bring up constraints, and allow them an opportunity to be recognized for their contribution.

Example of communication plan

Frequency	Audience	Message
Yearly	All IT employees	Current business strategy, constraints and impact on IT
Quarterly	All IT employees	Quarterly results (satisfaction, operations, projects) Success stories Areas needing attention Recognition Upcoming events
Monthly	All IT employees	Success stories
Monthly	Different group/team every month	Participation in their monthly meeting

Meeting tempo

Meetings are a necessary evil. Although they generally are a waste of time, we haven't found a better way to keep everyone informed and included in the decision-making process. But, if you are like most IT departments, the way you are running meetings today is just dreadful.

Most IT departments have a weekly status meeting, scheduled to last an hour but often taking much longer, where people share their status and discuss issues. The problem is that we often end up talking about specific projects or issues that concern only a handful of people in the room. Everyone else checks their e-mail or works on something else.

Can you turn these meetings into activities that will encourage participation and motivate the team? Yes, it is possible. The key is to replace the weekly status meeting with four distinct types of meetings.

The meeting tempo proposed below separates meetings by the level of detail the team needs to examine. A common mistake is mixing high-level concept meetings with deep-down operational matters. Everyone quickly starts discussing details and loses sight of the big picture. And, once you go down, it is very hard to go back up again. By separating these discussions into different meetings, we can keep the conversations focused on the topic at hand.

Meeting	Objective	Agenda
Weekly ops meeting (thirty minutes)	Review the operational performance for the previous week and identify issues.	Review late tickets Review availability Review project status Top three issues
Monthly direction meeting (ninety minutes)	Review quarterly objectives and strategies and assess evolution/completion.	Top five priorities status Budget Satisfaction score/issues Tickets
Quarterly strategic meeting (half-day)	Review past quarterly priorities and assess effectiveness. Develop new quarterly priorities. Review the status of each department/partners and review/set objectives.	Top five priorities review/status New top five priorities Top-down communication / vision Company direction/vision Account status
Yearly retreat (full day)	Review the priorities for the last year. Define new priorities for the year. Review high-level concepts like organizational structure, etc.	Role review Focus area

Does it sound like a lot? Actually, it is only ten hours more per year than your current method (sixty-two hours versus fifty-two hours for the weekly one-hour status meeting). Considering that the weekly meeting often lasts much longer, it is almost the same. But you do get much more value now. The weekly meeting, at only thirty minutes, no longer stops the week in its tracks. It is a quick meeting meant to talk about current issues and keep everyone in the loop. Specific issues needing to be discussed are sidelined, and special meetings are scheduled with only the relevant people, keeping the week's momentum going.

On the other hand, the more strategic monthly and quarterly meetings aim to look at services on a higher level and define and correct the orientations. Everyone receives an opportunity to talk about more fundamental issues. Finally, the yearly meeting gives the team a chance to look at the really big picture and address major orientations.

This meeting tempo keeps people more engaged and motivates them to be prepared and concise.

6. Goldilocks processes

Processes as a fence

We had just finished implementing an ERP in record time, but to do that, we had to compromise on many functionalities—and, by "compromise," I mean we did not do them at all. Of course, this had an impact on users' workload and productivity, but we promised them that, once the application was up and running, we would accept change requests.

So, after we finished implementing the ERP, the changes started to pour in. It was a deluge. We had hundreds of requests from various parts of the organization. Some asked for new reports, some asked for changes in the interface, and some asked for minor aesthetic adjustments. It became difficult to manage the sheer numbers of requests, let alone evaluate and prioritize them.

So, of course, I did what any IT department would do: I established a process. And a simple one, at that. The user had to submit a form with the proposed change, and we would evaluate it, prioritize it, and schedule it in an upcoming release. Easy enough—except that the submission form was four pages long.

It asked all sort of questions, such as, "What are the modules affected?", "What are the benefits?", and "Will it have an impact on other business units?" A lot of the questions were difficult or even impossible for the user to answer—and that was the point. I had established the process to act as a gatekeeper. It was a test of will to see if the change was really worthwhile. My thinking was: if a user commits to fill out a four-page form, then it must be valuable to the organization.

I didn't make a lot of friends with this form. But, sure enough, it worked. Requests started to slow down to a manageable level. I had built a process aimed at helping myself, not the users. I had also established myself as an obstacle, not a partner.

That seems to be the goal of a lot of processes established by IT departments. We use processes to manage the demand side of the supply-and-demand equation. But, as we'll see, Level 4 IT departments don't use processes as gatekeepers. They build Goldilocks processes: not too much, not too little.

How Level 4 IT departments create Goldilocks processes

Level 4 IT departments build Goldilocks processes in three ways:

- They simplify processes.
- They remove constraints.
- They avoid the process altogether.

1. Simplifying processes

Business units often ask for a new software or tool to automate a process. IT's reaction is always: "We can't just automate the existing way of doing things. We need to examine the entire process." And, of course, this thinking is correct. There is no point in doing the wrong thing faster. We need to take a long, hard look at why we are performing these activities in the first place. So, why is it that most IT departments don't follow their own advice?

Level 4 IT departments ask themselves four questions when looking at processes:

- Do we need it?

- What's the objective?

- What's the minimum we need to get started?

- How will we measure the process?

Question 1: Do we really need it?

A lot of the processes that IT departments everywhere have put in place have been reactive in nature. A problem showed up, someone decided we needed a new process to make sure it never happened again, and it was implemented. No one looked at the objectives behind it or even if the problem justified the creation of a new process to begin with. We often build processes just to deal with the odd exception.

Level 4 IT departments take a long, hard look at whether the process is even needed. In general, putting a process in place simply to deal with the odd exception wastes both time and resources. No process will be perfect, and exceptions will always exist, anyway. Trying to cover all possible scenarios and exceptions will result in a process that is heavy and complex. Unless the exception can lead to catastrophic consequences, processes are not needed.

Question 2: What is the objective?

The second question Level 4 IT departments ask themselves is "What's the objective?" In other words, what are we trying to do?

Processes have four different objectives:

- Productivity: Ensure that the information required is available. Aim to avoid back-and-forth communication that takes time and resources.

- Predictability: Make sure the task gets done properly and systematically (checklists, for example).

- Coordination: Ensure that different people's tasks are completed and in the right sequence.

- Control: Ensure the process is performed only if properly authorized.

Of course, a process might have more than one of these objectives. For example, the acquisition of new equipment might touch on all four. But, too often, we assume that all the objectives are required when that's not the case.

Let's take control, for example. How many of your processes currently need some kind of approval step? A manager or someone else needs to approve a request before a new piece of equipment or software is installed. But is that control step required? What would happen if we removed it? Would it cost a fortune?

One of my clients had a process in place that required manager approval for replacing small equipment (a computer mouse, for example). The financial impact of this was almost negligible. Even if every employee requested a new mouse every year, it would represent only 0.1 percent of the IT budget. The process required an approval step to protect against a nonexistent risk.

Level 4 IT departments review the objectives behind their processes and remove non-value-added steps without mercy. This makes the processes simpler and faster, saving time and money.

Question 3: What is the minimum we need to get started?
A lot of IT processes start with a form to be filled out by the user. Need a new computer? Fill out a form. Want a change to an

application? Fill out a form. Forms are everywhere when we think of IT processes. And, more often than not, the forms are too long.

It is easy to keep adding questions to a form. At a scheduled meeting, we ask, "What do we need to know to get this process going?" We then get the two or three critical pieces of information we need. But then, we keep adding: "It would be nice if we knew...." or "What if this rare exception happens, then we would need...." And the form keeps getting longer.

The problem with such forms is that not only are they tiresome to fill out, but they also contain fields that are irrelevant to most users. By trying to cover all exceptions, we're making the form unusable.

Level 4 IT departments ruthlessly question every field on their forms: "Do we really need to know this?" "What would happen if we removed this field?" As a result, they streamline the form to the point where it is concise, clear, and easy to fill out. In turn, the information it contains is of a higher quality.

Question 4: How will we measure the process?

How do you know if your process is working? Most IT departments simply move on to something else once the process is established. Did the process fix the problem? Probably. Is it efficient? There is no way to know for sure.

One of the first questions I ask IT leaders is, "How many support requests did you get this month?" I like this question because it tells me very quickly if the IT department has a good reputation and whether the IT leader is connected to its operations. Too often, the answer is, "I don't know. I'd have to ask."

If a process was important enough to be put in place, then it is important enough to be managed. Level 4 IT departments continually monitor the performance of their processes. They do so by using simple metrics:

- How many times did the process get triggered?

- How many times was there an exception to the process?

- Is the project achieving its objective?

Simply measuring the process keeps it clear to everyone involved, highlights whether it is working, and determines if it still makes sense.

Example: Support request form

The IT leader of a government agency complained that users kept calling the help-desk when they should be submitting requests through the web form or portal instead. She felt it would be easier to prioritize and manage resources if most of these requests came from the web form.

So, we went and looked at the ticket portal and found out why people didn't want to use it: it was too complex. It not only asked for a lot of information, but it also asked for information that was not always available or relevant. Users had to "guess" what to fill in, and more often than not, they entered whatever was easiest.

But how much of this information was necessary? We went to the support team and started talking with the staff. "How much of the information in the ticket do you really use?" we asked. As it turned out, they used little. To begin with, they already had most of the information in their support system. They didn't need users to tell them what OS or applications were installed; they knew this already. Most importantly: the users gave unreliable information. They often filled in whatever it took to get the form through. Because the information proved too unreliable for the technicians to take it for granted, they simply ignored it.

Working with the support team, we redesigned the form with only two fields: e-mail and a text box for users to describe their problem. And people connected to the portal already didn't even have to supply their e-mail because we already knew who they were.

A communication was sent out to showcase the new form and incite people to use it. Usage of the form increased significantly. But, most importantly, users no longer saw it as a barrier to interacting with IT.

Initial Request Form	Simplified Form
Name	E-mail
E-mail	How can we help you?
Phone	
Department	
Priority (low, medium, high)	
Description of the problem	
When you can be contacted	
Equipment	
Operating system	
Application	

2. Removing constraints

Most processes are built to accommodate a constraint. After all, if we possessed unlimited money, we wouldn't need to approve every employee expenditure. If we had unlimited software licenses, we wouldn't need to approve and install them. They would come in the base image. Such constraints are the reason we build processes in the first place.

But we tend to spend more time building processes than trying to remove the constraints. For example, ordering equipment is a major constraint. When we consider that the average internal cost of making a purchase is $429, issuing a PO for an item costing less wastes money and resources. This is why IT departments don't typically like making "one-of" purchases. However, we can easily remove this constraint by simply building a small inventory ahead of time. The cost of carrying the inventory is easily offset by the cost of procurement.

Approvals are the second constraint. We require the user's manager's approval before we install new software or new equipment. Why? In some cases, it is for budget control. The manager controls his or her budget and wants to make sure it isn't being spent on unnecessary items. But, most of the time, IT's budget is centralized. The managers suffer no consequences in approving or rejecting requests. IT demands the manager approve the request to prevent abuse, but it actually says to the user, "We don't trust your judgment." What if you were to remove the approval? Would the impact be so dramatic?

We performed the experiment with an organization of four thousand users. We removed all approvals from the new equipment and the software-approval processes. If you asked for it, then you got it. Of course, the IT team followed standards, but they were given discretion to bypass those standards if need be. The result? No changes in the budget. There were no more requests, and we couldn't find any frivolous expenditures. The approval processes provided protection against a risk that almost never happened.

Controls can be built in at the end of the process. Instead of blocking the process with approvals and gates, what if we simply built exception reports? An IT department decided to let employees use their mobile devices for personal use (which most did already, anyway). They negotiated great plans for voice and data and provided as much flexibility to the users as possible and as was financially responsible. But they also built exception reports. Every month, the employees who exceeded their plan received a notification. The second month, IT copied the manager on the note. Sometimes, these excesses were justified, and the manager simply ignored them. The few times in which the employees were actually abusing the policy entailed a discussion with their managers, and their behavior fixed itself naturally.

New hires

One of the common sources of dissatisfaction for both the business and IT is the new-hire process.

Setting up a new hire is a fairly complex process: we have to acquire and configure the equipment, determine where he or she will sit, define which access and which printers will be required, etc. Most often, the hiring manager has no idea of what is really needed and just ends up saying something along the lines of, "Give her the same access as John Doe."

The delay is the really frustrating part for everyone. IT is typically informed of a new hire at the very last minute (often the same day!). This leaves IT scrambling to procure, configure, and deploy equipment. And, of course, something is always missing—an access is not provided or simple problems arise from the rush job. This process leaves both IT and the business angry.

IT typically attempts to solve this problem by asking for a quicker heads-up and more time to prepare: "If the business could only give us a week's notice, then it would solve all our problems." We decipher complex forms and try to figure out all the equipment and access required. The business fills out the forms as best it can, but typically has no idea. And, most of the time, people simply forget the process, and we are back to the last-minute game again.

What if, instead of fighting the short delay, we made the most of it? We came up with one solution to solve the last-minute hire problem by setting up a "fifteen minutes" process. We asked ourselves: Can we provision a new computer in only fifteen minutes?

The idea was simple: You need a computer? You call the help-desk; they instruct you to go down to your site's reception area, where a computer waits for you. The help-desk configures live with you, and, within fifteen minutes, you are back to work.

Of course, that meant a lot of "IFs." The computers would need to be at the reception desk already, they would require some configuring, the help-desk would need the instructions and access to create and manage users, and most of the configuration must already have taken place.

We started by analyzing what it would take to support such a process and came up with some ingenious solutions. First, it meant that we needed to have the computers on-site already—not a small task when you consider we had twenty-two sites to support. To solve this issue, we asked the receptionist at each site to help us out. It also meant that we preconfigured all the computers with an image containing all the applications, network maps, Wi-Fi networks, printers, etc. Thus, the help-desk only had to remove unneeded applications and printers (a much faster process) rather than install everything (which can be time-consuming). If the new computer was an upgrade or an exchange, an online backup application would restore the backup over a day or two, in order of file last accessed. So chances were that, within minutes, the user had access to what he or she had been working on last on the old computer right away, while the older files were slowly restored.

Every time we handed a computer out, a new computer was ordered. We asked the supplier to image the computers themselves and ship them directly to the sites, taking all the technicians' time out of the process. We sent old computers out to be refurbished. If they were still good, then they were reimaged and put back into circulation or given to local nonprofits. The receptionist also carried a selection of mice, power adapters, keyboards, cables, and various accessories users might need on an ongoing basis. Thus, if a user needed a new mouse, he could simply head over to the receptionist and get one instantly.

How much did this cost? Not much, actually. Some would say that carrying an inventory of computers at each site would be very costly.

Let's do some quick math: twenty-two sites with five computers on standby at each site at $1,000 each equals $110,000. Because they would get used in the evergreening process, the real cost is simply that of carrying the inventory—let's say 10 percent interest per year, thus $11,000. Not bad for dramatically increasing user satisfaction.

IT no longer cared if new employees showed up without warning. In fact, it was now the procedure. We included a short training session on the process so that, when new employees arrived, we could set up their computer and provide them with some guidance on how to best use it, get support, etc. It gave us opportunities to positively interact with users for the first time, educate them a little bit, and follow-up a few days afterward to solve any issues and build credibility.

HR was ecstatic, the users were happy, and IT was no longer frustrated.

Processes built with the business in mind

One of my government clients was struggling with its project-intake process. Every year, it went through a capital-budgeting process that involved getting project requests from the business. Every year, it would receive between one hundred and two hundred requests. But this year was different—the government had gone through a massive restructuring, which severely reduced project budgets. In fact, several of the projects for the current year had been halted for lack of funding.

The relationship managers got nervous thinking about the deluge of initiatives and projects that would come from the business. They would have to evaluate and rank them, yet only a few would actually see the light of day. It would be an odious task.

The team debated the best way to address the situation. One solution was to make the intake process stricter, requiring longer forms and more justification of how the project benefited and aligned with the business. In other words, make the business work more. This would probably have worked to reduce the number of demands, but it would have tainted relationships in the process.

Instead, the team did something courageous: they cancelled the intake process. They took all the uncompleted projects from the previous year and used the same prioritization to compile a list of projects that should be done this year. Of course, there were more than enough projects on the list to fill the available capacity, and then some.

Then the team crafted a communication to the business leaders, reminding them of the financial situation and tell them that, as such, there would be no intake process. Instead, they recommended working on the identified initiatives based on last year's prioritization. They followed up with one-on-one meetings to provide an opportunity for the business leaders to voice their concerns and reprioritize projects if need be. Some did take the opportunity to reprioritize, and some even cancelled projects on the list, but the changes were minimal.

The entire process went very smoothly. The business leaders were happy to have avoided a pointless intake exercise. The IT department didn't have to evaluate new initiatives and could focus on delivery instead. The relationship managers were not in a situation in which they would have to say no to almost every new initiative.

3. Avoiding processes

We tend to take processes for granted. If it exists, then we must follow it. But sometimes, like our previous example in which no resources were available, the process just doesn't make sense anymore. Next year perhaps it will, if resources free up.

Level 4 IT departments always refer back to the objective of the process before engaging in it. If the objective, or circumstance, has changed, then it may be time to requisition the process itself.

But avoiding processes is not always an option. What Level 4 IT departments do instead is to make sure processes don't get triggered in the first place.

Avoiding the process altogether

The easiest process is no process at all. We save time and effort, and we also prevent the stakeholders from developing new expectations.

A good example of this is the project-approval process, which falls under most IT departments' governance. Projects follow the supply-and-demand equation: there is a fixed supply of money and resources available and a large demand for new initiatives. To cope with the demand, the process involves prioritizing the available resources to only the most important, strategic, and beneficial projects. The goal of the approval process is thus to cut as many projects as possible.

The typical process starts with a global call for new initiatives. The business is given a form to fill out for each new initiative it can think up. The form is long and complex, which acts as the first test of the governance process. If the business proves dedicated enough to complete the form, then the project must be worthwhile.

The projects are evaluated at a high level, giving a sense of what the project will look like in terms of cost and effort.

If costs make sense, the project then goes through a business case process. The benefits and costs are detailed to determine exactly how the project will contribute to the organization. The business case evaluates the return on investment and alignment with the organization's priorities.

Finally, projects are prioritized, and a line is drawn when we run out of money. If you are lucky, your project is above the line and will get done. If you are unlucky, your project is pushed to "another year," which basically means that it will never get done.

We call this process "the funnel." Several projects go in, few come out. Each step is designed to weed out projects that aren't aligned with the goals of the organization. It is particularly difficult for everyone involved. It forces the business to work on many different project submissions that will never see the light of day. It forces IT departments to evaluate several unclear requests. It is a lot of work and frustration—and for what benefit?

Level 1–3 IT departments execute 30 percent of the initiatives that get submitted to the governance process. Less than one-third of projects submitted see the light of day. That's a lot of work and grief for very little results.

But Level 4 IT departments see their funnel a little differently. It looks more like a tube than a funnel.

The vast majority of projects that enter the funnel get realized. That's not because they have more capacity to realize projects—far from it. The difference is that projects that don't stand a chance never make it to the submission phase in the first place.

Level 4 IT departments work on the demand side of the supply-and-demand equation. They make sure the business doesn't waste their time by submitting projects that won't get approved. How do they accomplish this?

They use an informal governance process before the real governance process kicks in. Their relationship with the business provides them with a continual view of its needs and priorities. They have candid conversations about each of these projects as the ideas happen.

It also lets them inform the business that its project stands little chance, saving time for everyone in the process. Of course, nothing prevents the business from submitting projects anyway, but at least it understands the real chances of project approval.

Governance becomes more of an administrative process than a prioritization. It is the final approval of a continual process of discovery and influence. By skipping the process altogether, Level 4 IT departments make it easier to submit projects and to prioritize them. The entire process is lighter, less onerous in terms of time (from both sides), and more satisfying.

Goldilocks: Not too much, not too little

The IT industry has been overwhelmed by process-driven approaches in the past few years: the Project Management Office (PMO), the Information Technology Infrastructure Library (ITIL), and the Capability Maturity Model (CMM). They all encourage us to believe that more is better. "Improve your level." "Become more mature." "If a little is good, more is better!"

The reality is that the amount of processes or levels of maturity make little difference. Although processes make projects easier to execute, it is the IT team's willingness to integrate and live the six factors on a day-to-day basis that makes a difference.

Let's now see how you can integrate these six factors into your own team.

Becoming Level 4: Goldilocks processes

It is always difficult to manage the equilibrium between providing great customer service and keeping control of standards. Some levels of processes and gatekeeping are necessary. How can you become a Level 4 IT department without losing control? The key is to focus on the Moments of Truth.

Not every interaction with a user is a Moment of Truth. A Moment of Truth happens only when the interaction might potentially leave a lasting impression, positive or negative. In general, Moments of Truth are associated with high-anxiety events. The users are stressed, facing a deadline or an unfamiliar situation, and the way you accompany them throughout this process will dictate how they see you in the future. As John Churtom Collins said: "In prosperity our friends know us; in adversity we know our friends."

We identified the four most common Moments of Truth and what you can do to make things simpler for users:

1. User onboarding (hiring)
2. Phone support
3. Equipment change
4. New system/process change

First Moment of Truth: Hiring

Changing jobs can be stressful. According to the Holmes and Rahe Stress Scale, changing to a different line of work (changing jobs) rates a 36. To give perspective, being dismissed from work is 47, and the death of a spouse is 100. So, although changing jobs isn't as stressful as experiencing sexual difficulties (39), it still causes high anxiety for new employees. Stress being cumulative, it doesn't take much to form a bad impression with new employees. Setting up a computer late or providing one that is missing cables or simply not working correctly on the first try can be enough.

When we run user-satisfaction surveys, we try to look at the correlation between years of service and satisfaction. Instinctively, we might think that new employees are more satisfied with IT services. After all, they haven't yet accumulated a lifetime of dealing with problems and issues with the IT organization. Yet, we find the opposite; new employees are less satisfied.

Think of your new-hire setup process. How often does it go smoothly? If you're like many IT departments, you hear about the new hire too late, and not everything is ready when the employee arrives.

System accesses are missing. And, chances are, the employee will run into many issues during the first two weeks, getting well-acquainted with the help-desk.

Employees want to be productive as quickly as possible. They want to access the systems and start getting acquainted with them. They want to know how to access their messages wherever they are. In short, they want to be an engaged user. So, how do we help them?

A systematic onboarding process can help users achieve that proficiency very quickly. New employees are eager to learn and tend to have more time in the first few days. IT can leverage this to facilitate their transition.

Below is an example of an onboarding process used by one of our clients. You will see that IT plays a key role in orienting the employee through the use of his or her equipment, common areas such as meeting rooms, devices, and printers. IT also performs the first help-desk call with the new hire to show them exactly what the interaction will be like. This process achieves three objectives: 1) it confirms that everything works for the employee, 2) it ensures that he or she will be off to a positive start, and 3) it sets expectations for the kind of service to expect in the future.

Timeline	Onboarding Item
Three days before arrival	Ensure equipment is ready and installed
	Ensure printers and other peripherals have been configured
	Ensure accesses have been granted in all major systems
	Schedule IT onboarding meeting
	Schedule relevant system training
First day	Thirty-minute onboarding meeting:
	- Review basics: login to computer, printing
	- Conference room basics (go in the conference room with them)
	- Mobile device basics
	- Clarify rules and responsibilities
	- Pretend call to the help-desk
	- Provide one-pager with key info
	- Provide training curriculum and schedule
	- Set expectations on service and response time
	- Token item with support number (mug, keychain, etc.)
Next day	- Follow-up call from same tech to see if everything is okay
Following days	- Training (web-based, formal, etc.)
One week	- Review user engagement in key systems
	- Follow-up with user

Although this process might seem time-consuming, it really involves approximately one hour of a technician's time—a small investment to start the relationship well. In addition, although performing it live really helps build a relationship, our client successfully used it over the phone as well for remote offices.

Second Moment of Truth: Phone support

IT leaders would prefer users to submit their issues either through a web portal or through e-mail. It is much easier to manage workloads with written requests than phone calls. So, why do the users keep calling?

Users prefer to call rather than e-mail for two reasons. First, the problem is urgent (at least for the user), and they need resolution right away. Second, the problem is too complex to properly explain in an e-mail. They simply don't know where to start and require the guidance of a technician to properly frame the issue. Users will typically use web forms or e-mails for more mundane or less urgent requests. After all, they don't like wasting their time on the phone, either. Thus, phone calls are generally a category apart in terms of support situations. Users need a quick resolution or require help right away. They may be under a deadline or making their own customers wait. They might have tried to solve the problem themselves already and are getting frustrated. Anxiety is high—the perfect definition of a Moment of Truth.

So, let's be honest. When is the last time you listened to support calls? If you are like the majority of IT leaders, never. You may have walked past the support group and overheard conversations, but you probably never took the time to listen to an entire call, either live or recorded. And when did you last call the help-desk yourself? It might have been awhile. You may have an assistant who does it for you, or you contact the manager directly. But doing so deprives you of an important opportunity to witness just how the team interacts with your users—an important Moment of Truth.

Users are looking for two things when they call the help-desk: reassurance that the person understands the problem and that IT will take charge of it UNTIL IT IS CORRECTED. Users are afraid that their call will get lost or that the technician, believing the problem has been solved, will close the call when the problem still exists.

The biggest complaint users have with help-desk support is courtesy. When we talk to the help-desk staff, they don't feel they are not being courteous. But they certainly expedite calls, and users perceive this as a lack of courtesy. Is the help-desk staff measured by the number of calls per day? If so, you may be part of the problem.

Third Moment of Truth: Equipment changes

Users are anxious for a few reasons, mainly due to the loss of productivity. An equipment change takes time, during which users cannot work. Still, that's not a big deal, and they can plan around it. The real issues are users' uncertainties about whether they will be able to work AFTER a replacement. Equipment changes will inevitably bring problems: a printer not mapped, applications missing, Wi-Fi passwords disappearing, personal files and documents gone, etc. Users are also uncertain about their files, songs, videos, and web applications, which IT might not be aware of. "Will I lose them?" is a common concern.

We can facilitate this Moment of Truth in a few ways.

First, set expectations as to what will happen. A communication, video, or even presentation helps users greatly understand the entire process, what potential problems may happen, and what kind of support they will receive afterward. Technicians can make personal visits to identify any potential issues and address the users' questions and concerns. This goes a long way in helping users feel they are in control of the process and not simple victims. Scheduling the change in advance also allows the user to voice any concerns. Perhaps the timing isn't right (end of month, upcoming meeting, etc.), and rescheduling will reduce anxiety significantly.

The actual replacement leaves the user idle, either waiting for the process to complete or simply wandering the halls in search of something to do. Providing web access via temporary computers will at least allow users to conduct their most urgent business. It will also relieve the pressure technicians feel by having users nervously watching over their shoulders. People's computers are incredibly personal, and users hate having someone sifting through their files and information. They almost feel as if their private lives have been violated. Although you could assert that their work computers are company property, it is easier to simply acknowledge this feeling and minimize the actual interactions with the computer (through automation, for example).

To reassure users that they are not on their own and will not have to chase IT if something is left unfinished, a technician should be present the first time someone uses new equipment. The user can then, alongside the technician, test all major functionalities (printing, Internet, etc.) and software to ensure all is working as specified.

A personal follow-up a few days later helps identify any lingering issues that may have crept up or been missed in the tests. This proves especially useful for small issues that aren't worth a call to the help-desk but could become dissatisfiers. It also demonstrates that you assume responsibility up to the end; the user won't be left high and dry, with a new machine, if something happens.

Some IT departments treat hardware changes as a project, replacing a significant portion of their users' computers at one time. This is incredibly disruptive for the organization, as it suddenly affects productivity everywhere. IT's workload piles so high that it becomes difficult to provide adequate service, leaving both users and IT dissatisfied. Until the day arrives in which we no longer have to replace computers, it is best to treat it as a continuous process, performing the activity throughout the year in a controlled manner.

Some might view this Moment of Truth and find the approach excessive. After all, changing computers is not rocket science. However, our user-satisfaction surveys indicate that users remain systematically dissatisfied with this process, to the point where they'd rather extend the life of their old computer than go through this exchange. Even the promise of faster, better equipment fails to convince them. The problem, of course, is not that users don't want better equipment; they simply don't trust IT to do its job correctly.

Timeline	Equipment Change Step
One week prior	Presentation of the equipment-change process Schedule meeting with user Technician's visit to assess computer and identify specific needs
Day of the change	Provide temporary computer/equipment Perform change Test new equipment with the user
Two days after	Technician follow-up to address any lingering issues

Fourth Moment of Truth: New system/process change

The last Moment of Truth brings the most anxiety. Deploying new systems and processes typically facilitates major changes in the way people work, leading to job security worries and performance anxiety ("Will I be able to learn the new process?"). All of this combined rates pretty high on the anxiety scale.

Delivering a new business project is already very complicated. Development and configuration bring risks and issues, managing the schedule and its impact on the project is a logistical nightmare, and developing all of the training and documentation required is time-consuming. Projects take up enough time without worrying about user anxiety. After all, isn't change management HR's responsibility?

As it turns out, there is an important thing we can do to ease user anxiety during a project. We've been talking about user involvement for years, and it has always been a difficult subject. The business, already stretched, has few people to loan out to a project. Involving users can quickly become costly or difficult, with no guarantee that they will have the time or the skills to properly inform and prepare their own organization. Too often, IT focuses on training and neglects to manage change properly.

When we talk about user involvement, we usually mean active involvement—the users actually working on the project. But what about passive involvement?

Passive involvement is an incredibly efficient, easy, and overlooked way to manage change with the users. As we've seen throughout this book, managing expectations is a key element of managing business value. We've found that simply showing demos, screenshots, and videos of the new software in action goes a long way toward reducing anxiety. It is hard to be optimistic about something we know nothing about. Seeing how the forthcoming system works helps people visualize the process, adjust their expectations accordingly, and achieve more satisfaction when the system actually goes live.

Build processes around Moments of Truth
The overall theme of these Moments of Truth is very simple: accompany the users. Self-service and automated processes work great for low-value interactions and common, mundane requests. But, when users feel anxious and stressed, nothing compares to being able to rely on another human being. Simply knowing that they do not stand alone and that someone will guide them through to the end is an amazing way to reduce anxiety and leave a positive impression.

Simon Chapleau

Doing so requires resources. A technician who accompanies users through a computer replacement won't be able to complete as many per day compared to simply switching hardware and moving on. Although this method will have a short-term impact on productivity and performance metrics, the long-term benefits easily outweigh the costs.

The Value Creation Engine

Simple, but hard

Losing weight is simple: eat less and exercise more. But "simple" doesn't mean "easy." Over 33 percent of adults in the United States are considered obese. The problem is that losing weight requires changing our daily habits—preparing healthy meals or making the effort to exercise. It is much easier to eat fast food and watch television. We've ingrained ourselves in dozens of unhealthy habits that are hard to unwire, and we've developed an entire lifestyle around them.

But it can be done.

It is not something we can treat as a project—do once and move on. As people who have succeeded in losing weight will attest, it requires a daily commitment, focus, and dedication. There is no end line.

The project with no end date

Becoming a Level 4 IT department is a lot like losing weight. It's a project without an end date that requires a major shift in culture and daily habits. Everything, from our hiring profiles to our workloads and resource constraints nudges us toward our bad habits. It is much easier to go with the flow; something will always be more urgent or pressing.

In my consulting and workshops, I chart a comprehensive Business Value Engine Plan with my clients. This has helped them develop into Level 4 IT departments while still accomplishing their day jobs. I understand that, whatever you do, you still must run operations, execute projects, and deliver on all your commitments. This is why we've developed a plan that is light, requiring a minimum of effort but a lot of commitment. Because I can't be with you, what follows is a Business Value Engine Plan crash course, condensed into a manageable process for you and your team.

Before you get ready, here are a few housekeeping items to keep in mind. First, although this project has no end date, it is still useful to treat it as a project. It is not overly taxing, but it requires some time and effort be set aside. And from experience, it might never get done if there is no deadline. Something more "urgent" always calls. Next, your team will test your commitment to this. They will try to "wait you out" to make sure it is not simply the new flavor of the day. Finally, progresses, even small ones, need to be celebrated. Ideally, with pizza, but that's just me.

The Value Creation Engine

The Value Creation Engine contains three steps and takes anywhere from six to twelve months to complete. But, contrary to many transformation plans, the Value Creation Engine front-loads the benefits early in the plan. This means you don't have to wait months or years to start seeing benefits.

The plan has three phases:

- Phase 1: Start the engine
- Phase 2: Accelerate

- Phase 3: Cruise control

Phase 1: Start the engine

One of the most common pitfalls of value creation plans is starting with an in-depth analysis phase. Although analysis is important, it is like sitting in a rocking chair: it gives us something to do but gets us nowhere.

In this phase, our objective is to create momentum and get the ball rolling. One of the best ways to do this is to create urgency. As we have learned before, it is important to move value creation activities from the important-nonurgent quadrant into the important-urgent one to attract the attention of managers and staff. We will do this by employing the user-satisfaction survey as the trigger for change.

Step 1. User-satisfaction surveys

Performing user-satisfaction surveys is both easy and inexpensive. You can do them internally using the available web tools or contract an outside firm to do it, providing confidentiality to the respondents. Our own research and experience have taught us that surveys should be kept short (within ninety seconds) and focus on the essentials.

Administering the survey once is not enough. To really start the engine, you should conduct the survey every month, sending it to different groups of users so that no one receives a survey more than once or twice a year. Each segment should represent the overall population of users. Using this frequency of survey, we can start treating user satisfaction as a key performance indicator (KPI). The survey report (at least the executive summary) should be distributed to the entire team and included in your own monthly KPI dashboard.

This will instantly raise not only the team's awareness of user satisfaction but also its level of importance. As we've said, what interests my boss fascinates me. If you look at satisfaction numbers every month, everyone will stay more attuned to it.

Step 2. Evaluate your team

Perhaps you already did the exercise when you read Chapter 5 "Fewer but Better." If not, now is the time to evaluate your team's technical, business, and behavioral competencies. In the next phase, you will dole out more responsibility and accountability to your team members, and it is important to know if they can handle it.

This evaluation will also analyze the level to which you trust every team member. Together, they will answer a critical question: do you have the right team? We often see IT leaders start a transformation program only to halt it when they realize they need to change some key people. Of course, by then it is too late for retraining. Doing an early analysis gives you a chance to develop a remediation plan for the problematic individuals.

Step 3. Develop partnerships plans

We've seen in the chapter on building partnerships that such plans are built in three steps: 1) understand, 2) set objectives, and 3) manage. We propose that you perform the first step (i.e. understand) for each of your business units.

This exercise will highlight two things: 1) which business units you already enjoy a good relationship with and which ones you know little about, and 2) what information you are missing to make a comprehensive plan. These exercises are always an eye opener for the IT team members, making them realize just how little they know about the business. But we want this experience to be positive, not negative. You must follow it with specific actions to fill that gap.

Step 4. Set up a dissatisfiers fighting squad

You can make a major impact on user satisfaction, very quickly, simply by removing the dissatisfiers and the irritants that plague the lives of your users. The user-satisfaction survey will have already disclosed a few issues through user comments. You can complement this with a dissatisfiers fighting squad, a group of technicians who identify and remove the little annoyances.

They will accomplish this by starting with the common areas, such as departmental printers and conference rooms. We've already seen a list of the common dissatisfiers to track. The squad is responsible for identifying, eliminating, and ensuring that these dissatisfiers don't return. Of course, this isn't a full-time role, but it will require some time, and the expectations should be very clear.

Step 5. Involve yourself in operations

Building value is about changing culture, not processes. To change culture, you will have to get your hands dirty and get involved in the day-to-day support activities. One way to do this is to block time on your calendar—a half-hour or an hour every week—to review operational performance. And by this, I don't mean simply reviewing KPIs, but getting deep in the operations.

Support tickets are a good starting point. If you don't have access to the support system, I suggest you create a user ID right away, then learn how to navigate the system and view the status of tickets. You should be most interested in the old tickets. Tickets more than a week old should include an explicit action plan that explains why. If not, add your own comments to the ticket to find out. Nothing motivates support technicians to resolve an issue like having their IT leader get directly involved in their tickets.

The goal is not to harass or punish the support team; their job is hard enough. It is simply to send the message that support is important and that you do monitor it. It will also give you a feel for the tone of the conversations, how technicians interact with users, and whether these are appropriate.

Step 6. Set up your new meeting tempo

Unfortunately, meetings drive a lot of what we are doing. If not for meetings, people would never read reports or analyze their performance. Meetings provide natural deadlines for people to do their work and prevent them from being entirely consumed by day-to-day activities.

But meetings should help motivate people, not the opposite. We suggest you implement the meeting tempo discussed in the "Fewer but Better" chapter:

- Weekly thirty-minute meetings to review operations

- Monthly ninety-minute meetings to review objectives, status, and accounts

- Quarterly half-day meetings to review and set objectives

- Annual off-site meetings to discuss strategies and orientations

If it doesn't get scheduled, it doesn't get done. Go ahead and schedule these meetings for the next eighteen months, then be intransigent with respect to the purpose of the meeting. Sideline any irrelevant discussions and stay focused on the agenda. And most importantly: respect the time. When it is up, stop the meeting, no matter what, even if you must interrupt someone. This will show your commitment to running a tight ship.

But I don't have time for this!

Of course you don't. No one has the time to take on any additional work. We work long hours as it is—why take on any more work? The reality is that you will need to make the time. If you feel that this work is too "operational" and not "strategic" enough, then I will simply refer you back to the IT Value Hierarchy: you cannot play a higher-level role if your Basics are not covered.

Phase 2: Accelerate

In Phase 1, our objective was to start the engine. In this phase, the goal is to accelerate to achieve rapid gains.

Why is it so important to act quickly? Simply, it is because of inertia: an object at rest will tend to stay at rest, while an object in motion will tend to stay in motion. In this phase, it is very easy for everyone to simply revert back to his or her old ways. New projects appear or crises come up, and what was once urgent suddenly becomes less so. But if we can build sufficient momentum, our new plan will take a life of its own that will take considerable effort to stop.

Step 1. Develop user personas

You have been receiving user-satisfaction survey results for a few months by now. You should have a pretty good idea of who is satisfied and who isn't, which provides a great starting point for developing user personas. As we've seen, user personas categorize users based on how they use technology and will allow you to customize your services to better meet user needs.

Once personas are defined, it is a matter of adapting the equipment and technology to fit their needs. Does the Excel-jockey have the big screens he or she needs? Does the traveling engineer have a robust laptop that works in freezing cold and can be bumped around? Of course, you will probably not be in a position to replace everyone's equipment at once, and that's not the goal. The goal is to develop new standards for future equipment and start testing them. Appoint a few representatives from each group and involve them in the new-equipment selection process.

Step 2. Measure engagement

Providing access to systems is no longer enough. We need to ensure that users are actually involved in the system. Now is the time to start developing engagement metrics. We've seen several metrics that can be used for this, but the easiest are typically the number of times people login to the system. This information is usually readily available, and its meaning is consistent from one system to another.

By looking at the usage patterns, given the user personas developed earlier, it is possible to identify the high-involvement group and the low-involvement group. This provides a starting point to analyze why some users are more or less involved in the system and allows you to implement action plans to increase engagement. By tracking engagement on a monthly basis, you can evaluate the effectiveness of these plans and correct them if need be.

Step 3. Training

Providing training will probably be one of the steps of the engagement plan set up previously. But training should also be provided for Basic services, such as office tools and e-mail. Users should be able to confidently use technology in order to become more autonomous and willing to depend on technology for other aspects of their work.

The easiest training sessions to provide at first are lunch-and-learns. Set up a day every month to cover basic office productivity topics and invite users. At first, there might be only a few attendees, but don't get discouraged. Provide pizza—that gets people coming. As the users see the value in this training, they will show up in larger audiences.

These lunch-and-learns also make great forums to identify topics for the next session. Ask users what their pain points are. Chances are, you will get a long list of topics. Your satisfaction surveys, support ticket data, and engagement data will provide the rest.

Step 4. Communication plan

Believe it or not, users want to hear from you—and not just for system outages. They are interested in your performance, in the projects you are working on, and in upcoming events.

You communication plan should include various approaches that match different personas' preferences. A Facebook page or a tweet is a great way to reach the younger generation (at least, it was at the time of writing this book), while e-mail may be preferred by people on the road, and some might like to watch a video. Be ready to communicate your message through many different platforms and channels.

But what to say? Develop a communication schedule that includes pertinent information such as system interruptions, upcoming events and training, hints and tips, case studies, and your vision for the future.

Step 5. Track your Moments of Truth

By now, you should have a pretty good idea of your Moments of Truth, the key interactions that can potentially change a user's perception of IT's value. So, let's start tracking them. As we've discussed, not every interaction is a Moment of Truth. We often review post-ticket surveys to ensure that a specific interaction was adequate, and generally the results of these small surveys are very high. But, when we start analyzing them only for Moments of Truth, we see a different story.

Look at your Moments of Truth and start compiling data that represent how well you performed. Whether surveys or simply delays in closing tickets, any metrics here can help monitor these critical interactions.

Step 6. Schedule partnership-review meetings

Partnership-review meetings are a great way to facilitate open discussions on the value IT provides for each business unit, but it is not natural for many IT leaders to talk only about the service they provide and not about specific projects. This meeting focuses only on the relationship between IT and the business unit. Using the agenda provided in the partnership chapter makes the conversation easier.

Start by scheduling a quarterly meeting with your key stakeholders for the next eighteen months. Scheduling far in advance will ensure that you commit to the process and will also prevent the infamous "my calendar is full" excuse from the stakeholders. Don't feel quite ready to tackle all of the business units at once? Then start with your best business unit, your worst business unit, and the business unit you have no relationship with. This will cover all possibilities and make all subsequent meetings much easier.

Phase 3: Cruise control

Once enough momentum has been created, the goal is to operationalize value creation. Phase 1 and Phase 2 were relatively easy in terms of motivation. After all, they were simply treated as projects with specific objectives and end dates. However, this one is about continuity, about integrating new practices into the organization. In short, it is about changing the culture.

Changing a culture is no easy feat. In this case, we are asking people who have worked a certain way for years to simply change how they work—to stop focusing on technology and focus on the users and to stop relying on processes and rely, instead, on competencies. There is no longer a wrong and a right way of doing things. Now, every action needs to be adapted to the person and to the context, which can make managing a lot more difficult.

Considerations
As we've often said, this plan is easy, but hard. It requires constant dedication and focus. Changing daily behaviors is difficult. To help you along, we'd like to complete this section with three pieces of advice.

First piece of advice: Choose your metrics wisely
Metrics are an essential part of any transformation program. Without metrics, we are simply driving in the dark. We might be

covering many miles, but we don't really know if we're heading in the right direction (or if we'll run into a tree). We have a tendency to use the metrics that are easy to gather, not the ones we necessarily need.

Metrics should be chosen with the objective in mind. We usually set three objectives for metrics:

- Inform. Keep someone updated on the status of a situation. A project's status metrics can act as an early warning for senior management.

- Change a perception. Someone might have a false or biased view of a situation, and metrics can help correct that view. A metric that tracks service availability can change the perception that the server is always down.

- Change a behavior. Use metrics to encourage someone to change how he or she acts—using satisfaction metrics to incite help-desk agents to spend more time with users, for example.

Depending on the objectives you want to achieve, you may choose a different set of metrics altogether. It is thus normal that metrics will evolve over time to meet your new objectives.

Second piece of advice: Focus on culture, not process

It is a well-known fact in marketing that, when people call or e-mail your organization, you have five minutes to get back to them. Past that, you lose the opportunity to satisfy or engage them, and they move on to other things. After I explained that to an IT department, they tweaked their support system to automatically send an e-mail right after receiving a request. Their system even sent e-mails when people phoned in and left a voicemail, using the call-back number to track the user down. It was a pretty clever setup. Unfortunately, it missed the point entirely.

IT is obsessed with processes, but you cannot automate relationships. There is no way to design a process that can replace personal interaction with the users. Although self-service and automation have their place, they can quickly become barriers to building relationships.

The Value Creation Engine aims to build this interaction. But to do so takes time and effort. Processes can support these interactions, but they cannot replace them. So, don't be surprised if your team's first instinct is to take these steps and try to automate them as much as possible. "What if we built a dashboard that compiled partnership plans automatically?" Great, but it's the act of building the partnership plan that generates value, not the plan itself. Building the plan forces the relationship manager to reconsider each relationship, to determine if each relationship remains at the same level or if it has degraded, and to truly understand each department's priorities.

Too much automation and too many processes can dilute the value of the entire exercise.

Third piece of advice: Assign clear ownership

If you've ever attended a first-aid class, you probably remember one of the surprising lessons of people in groups. First-aid classes consistently teach us to never ask a group for help—it simply doesn't work. It is not because people are mean or voyeuristic; it is simply that no one in a group feels concerned individually. "Someone else will do it." No, you need to point to an individual, ask for his name, and then instruct him clearly that he is to call for help and get back to you. Without this clear delegation and ownership, no one will go ahead and call.

The same applies to your team. If you don't assign a clear owner to each activity's introductory plan, they will never get done. How many IT managers have been frustrated by their team's inability to tackle a program or to make changes, simply because team members lacked clear ownership?

Every task, activity, and objective should have a clear owner, a sense of its priority with respect to everything else, and a deadline. Without that, it is merely a suggestion.

Dealing with setbacks

There is an expression that says: "You know who your friends are when you are down." This has never been as true as it was for Mike.

A client of mine—we'll call him Mike—had established himself as an Agent, a true partner to the business. IT had a great reputation amongst the different business units. One of the ways it accomplished this was by compromising its development methodology to meet marketing's tight deadlines. A volatile marketplace required IT to move quickly and occasionally skip quality assurance and testing, which, of course, created major issues for finance. But everyone was a good corporate citizen who understood the sacrifices needed in the name of meeting deadlines. Until the day the system crashed.

A major technical issue happened, resulting in two days of downtime, right at the beginning of a new campaign. The organization lost revenues, of course, but it also lost a lot of credibility with its customers.

What once had been a team environment with a strong sense of camaraderie quickly became a wolf's den. Everyone turned his or her back on IT, even marketing. They blamed IT's methodology and the fact that IT failed to do enough testing.

Over lunch, Mike told me, "If I had known, I would have never agreed to speed things up. I would have let marketing fail." Of course, that's not a real option, either.

We like to think that partnerships evolve in only one direction: for the better. But the reality is that partnerships vary over time. At best, partnerships are only temporary. Events, crises, and promotions change partnerships over time. What Mike failed to realize is that he had ceased to be an Agent for quite some time. He had become a Butler, agreeing to what the business wanted. He had agreed to compromise his processes and quality, without having time to catch up, to the point where doing so was now normal. He wasn't playing his role.

You will encounter setbacks as you execute your Value Creation Engine. Some partnerships will grow, and some will fail. Some months, the users' satisfaction scores will be going down instead of up. During these times, it will be tempting to simply abandon the plan, to stop measuring and isolate IT from the organization once more. But it's during these times that you demonstrate to your team, and to the business, that you understand what being a partner is all about and that you refuse to give up.

Conclusion

You probably started this book thinking we would talk about high-level strategic thinking. That we would discuss topics such as governance, business architecture, and value streams. That we would examine how IT can empower the business and help set strategic direction. Instead, we talked about how it is important to take care of the computers and deliver great support, and that spending time in the field is critical. We went from a CIO wearing three-piece suits to one wearing steel-toed boots.

And this is what I hope you will retain from this book: delivering business value is a lot of mundane work. No one delivers value with strategic plans and high-level thinking. Value comes from actually understanding your customers, and helping them reach their goals.

Managing business value is not sexy. It is a lot of hard work and requires many discussions with people that would simply prefer we returned to the basement we came from. But forcing those conversations is necessary and a critical part of building value.

Managing business value is not strategic either—at least, not strategic in the sense we like to think about. No fancy PowerPoint decks or value stream diagram can replace delivering basic services well. It requires a constant focus and vigilance on your operations.

I hope this book inspired you to start your own Value Creation Engine. Stay in touch, visit **GreenElephantTeam.com/bvit** for templates, articles, and research to help you along, and subscribe to our mailing lists to be informed of new insights and tools. I'd also love to answer your questions or simply hear about your own experience. Please e-mail me at simon@greenelephantteam.com.

About the Author

Simon Chapleau is the founder of Green Elephant (www.GreenElephantTeam.com), a company that works with internal service providers around the world to help them deliver amazing value to their internal clients.

He won the Octas in 2010 for the enterprise project of the year, and he holds master's degrees in project management and marketing as well as an MBA. He is currently working hard to finish his doctorate with the Edinburgh Business School.

Simon regularly speaks at conferences around the world. He also delivers Green Elephant programs to private clients.

Prior to founding Green Elephant, Simon was CIO for Sanimax, a large North American recycling company. He has also been involved in several business transformation projects with major clients such as Allstate, Procter and Gamble, and ING as a director for Gartner, a leading IT management consulting firm.

Simon lives in Montreal with his wife and daughter.

www.ingramcontent.com/pod-product-compliance
Lightning Source LLC
Chambersburg PA
CBHW051906170526
45168CB00001B/265